Margaret Stewart Barbour Simpson

Helps to Make Ideals Real

Margaret Stewart Barbour Simpson

Helps to Make Ideals Real

ISBN/EAN: 9783337028794

Printed in Europe, USA, Canada, Australia, Japan

Cover: Foto ©ninafisch / pixelio.de

More available books at **www.hansebooks.com**

HELPS TO MAKE
IDEALS REAL

BY

Mrs. A. R. SIMPSON

AUTHOR OF
"THE SCOTTISH SONGSTRESS"
"FRIENDS AND FRIENDSHIP" ETC.

> "*Teacher, I find that since I have imbibed the teachings of the New Testament I can look beyond the mean gains of this life. I suppose the reason why English artists put so much perspective into their drawings is because Christianity has given them a Future, and the reason why Oriental artists fail to do so is because Buddha and Confucius do not raise the eye above the present.*"—JAPANESE ART STUDENT.

EDINBURGH & LONDON
OLIPHANT ANDERSON & FERRIER
1896

TO

THE WORLD'S

STUDENT CHRISTIAN FEDERATION

CONTENTS

CHAP.		PAGE
I.	THE VISION OF THE IDEAL	9
II.	THE ASCENT BEGUN	12
III.	HELPS AND HINDRANCES	15
IV.	THE IDEAL OF THE PILGRIM SPIRIT	20
V.	AN IDEAL REALISED—FRANCES RIDLEY HAVERGAL	26
VI.	,, ,, —REGINALD RADCLIFFE	31
VII.	THE QUEST OF THE IDEAL—IN MEMORY	39
VIII.	,, ,, ,, —IN MONEY	45
IX.	,, ,, ,, —IN TIME	52
X.	,, ,, ,, —IN BOOKS	58
XI.	THE MISSIONARY IDEAL	67
XII.	THE IDEAL IN FELLOWSHIP	76
XIII.	THE IDEAL IN SUFFERING	81
XIV.	BEHOLDING OUR IDEAL	86
XV.	THE IDEAL LIFE	91

CHAPTER I

THE VISION OF THE IDEAL

> "Still, through our paltry stir and strife,
> Glows down the wished Ideal,
> And Longing moulds in clay what Life
> Carves in the marble Real!"

> "The true ideal is not opposed to the real, nor is it any artificial heightening thereof, but lies in it, and blessed are the eyes that find it."—LOWELL.

NOT long ago we read this sentence in a letter of a friend from Florence, "I can see sunshine gilding the distant heights, but I am standing at the very foot." The same winter, when walking in the outskirts of our city, an errand-boy passed us, basket on arm. He ran on in front, and every now and then rested his notebook on the wall to draw pictures. He also had an ideal. Bishop Westcott says: "The vision of the Ideal guards monotony of work from becoming monotony of life." We may smile at our children on the nursery floor enacting the scenes of daily life, the buying and selling, the borrowing and lending; but were our thoughts laid open, how many of our castles in the air have also as yet "no ladders to earth." We are in our turn seeking to imitate the great and the good, whose inspiration we have caught.

Prose and Poetry, Painting and Sculpture are full of the thought of the ideal in the different stages of growth; and what makes us see and find the longing for it everywhere, is that we feel the stirrings of it in ourselves. Never war-horse pawed the ground more restlessly, never bird beat against the bars of its cage more ceaselessly, than does the spirit of man strive within him. We cannot always analyse or define this indefinable something, this ambition, aspiration, longing, yearning of the spirit. Augustine has said: "Thou madest us for Thyself, and our hearts are not at rest, until they repose in Thee;" though some are led by slow stages to find this out. The growth of the ideal is like a painting, which we reproduce (p. 38), of an old woman with a bundle on her back, climbing the stairs in an Edinburgh "Close." The lowest steps may be duty, the love of hard work, the blessing of the text, "In the sweat of thy face shalt thou eat bread." The highest is surely the vision of God through His Son: "We beheld His glory." Some have gone through the pages of Amiel's Journal, ascending and descending with that idealist in his varying moods, of whom a critic says: "I fear that his malady of the Ideal was a compound of pride and sloth. He was so much afraid of doing anything imperfectly, that he did nothing at all. Moreover, his was the ideal of the imagination chiefly; it had not in it that urgent sense of duty which compels a man to do his best, even when the poverty of his doings pains him." We come back from his sometimes stimulating, sometimes saddening pages, more thankful than ever for the old Scotch Paraphrase which we heard sung in our youth in cottars' houses among the peatmoss on the heather-moors, by godly souls, unlearned in Amiel, but learned in this—

> "O may Thy Spirit seal our souls,
> And mould them to Thy will,
> That our weak hearts no more may stray,
> But keep Thy precepts still;
>
> That to perfection's sacred height
> We nearer still may rise,
> And all we think, and all we do,
> Be pleasing in Thine eyes."

For we like to think of this life being an ascent toward the prize of the "upward calling." And even though when one height is scaled it be but to find another, it is ever better on before. The higher we go, the air is clearer, the prospect is wider, the views are more bewitching. Some one may say, We do not want bright visions in the clouds, but footpaths in our daily life. Yet the vision helps the climber. One cannot do another's climbing, but one can help some young mountaineer to take the start heavenward. We would like to get the knapsack, the field-glass, the alpenstock ready. We may be able to clear away some hindrances because we have passed that way ourselves. Some of our own experience, for example, we try to throw into the following chapters. "If we cannot realise our ideal, we can at anyrate idealise our real;" and we give glimpses of two champions whose ideal is now realised, for they have reached the summit and entered the eternal Hospice. On their staff we do not read the name of any highest Alp, but "He led them forth by the right way, that they might go to a city of habitation."

The vision of those who have attained lures us on, and we feel that for those above also there is progress. Sometimes they seem so near that we are almost within hearing of their call, within sight of their beckoning, so great is the pressure of the spirit world.

> "A good man, and an angel! these between
> How thin the barrier! What divides their fate?
> Perhaps a moment, or perhaps a year.
> Angels are men in lighter habit clad,
> High o'er celestial mountains wing'd in flight;
> And men are angels, loaded for an hour,
> Who wade this miry vale, and climb with pain
> And slippery step, the bottom of the steep."

CHAPTER II

THE ASCENT BEGUN

"The situation that has not its Duty, its Ideal, was never yet occupied by man. Yes, here in this miserable, despicable Actual, wherein thou even now standest,—here or nowhere is thy Ideal! Work it out therefrom! . . . The Ideal is in Thyself; the impediment, too, is in Thyself!"—CARLYLE.

"Jesus presented to the world a solitary Ideal, and in innumerable lives has made it real."—JOHN WATSON.

> "Behind my back I fling, like an unvalued thing,
> My former self and ways;
> And reaching forward far, I seek the things that are
> Beyond time's lagging days."

IN our frontispiece, from the pencil of Mrs. Munro Ferguson, we see a climber who has fairly started. It seems strange that, in the most important matter of our life, for time and eternity, some do not show even the ordinary earnestness and precision with which they would make arrangements for a summer holiday. The text runs: "Shall two walk together except they have made an appointment?"—and all through Scripture there is the call and the choice, the opportunity and the decision. We know how tourist offices are besieged when a steamer is to leave any port, and how the coupons are carried carefully in the breast-pocket. The sleepy travellers in a hotel at a mountain foot know well by the early knock, and the heavy steps on the wooden stairs, that an expedition has been planned. In the fresh morning air the company is on foot, and the sleepers sleep on. The climbers were in earnest, made a plan, kept to it, and started.

"Nothing happens," says one; and yet many speak as if some day, somehow, they would awake to find themselves saved. Not so Peter, who says: "Give diligence to make your calling and election sure." In engaging a courier or guide for a holiday tour, the agreement is sometimes in writing; and in the quiet of our own chamber we can to-night put to our seal that God is true. Was it a stormy night, with the wind howling outside, when Christ said to Nicodemus: "The wind bloweth where it listeth, and thou hearest the voice thereof, but knowest not whence it cometh, and whither it goeth: so is every one that is born of the Spirit?" Nicodemus heard and obeyed; and the blessed Spirit is working still, whether, as like a summer breeze, He gently calls the child Samuel in the stillness of the night, or as the bursting of a cyclone, He lays down Saul prostrate at the midday hour. The Holy Spirit is the Guide, the Revealer.

He taught John to say: "A new commandment write I unto you, which thing is true in Him and in you; because the darkness is passing away, and the true light already shineth." In Him and in you; you may make of the commandment a covenant. In Him first, who cannot lie, and in you because you believe His word. You have seen the vision; the Spirit leads you through the Son to the Father; the Ideal has dawned on your gaze, and you exclaim: "This God is our God for ever and ever: He will be our guide even unto death." "See," saith the Spirit, "that thou make all things according to the pattern shewed to thee in the Mount."

The Swiss guide has to see that everything needful is provided, and disposes of all impediments. Miss Havergal says that in her climbing it made all the difference when the guide was obeyed implicitly, and her steps went just where his had been. "Thorough knowledge of the guide's language adds both to the enjoyment and safety of our following. . . . The guide decides your rest as well as your progress. . . . A Swiss guide is literally faithful unto death." Her lovely imagination and Spirit-taught soul found meaning everywhere, even in the coil of rope with its scarlet line. Other mountaineers tell us how different are the steps of an amateur and of an expert. Slow and steady are the guide's steps. He does not hurry, nor does he loiter. As there was the decision at the first, so there must be the purposeful march all through. How much easier it would seem in our climbing after our Ideal, if sometimes we might rush on. And again, we would fain linger and have the luxury of looking back, till Paul's words make us take heart again, and we forget the things that are behind—

> "Be it mine
> One aim to cherish and to track one line,
> Straight on to heaven to press with single bent;
> To know and love my God, and then to die content."

CHAPTER III

HELPS AND HINDRANCES

> "Make straight paths for your feet."—HEB. xii. 13.
> "An highway shall be there, and a way, and it shall be called The way of Holiness."—ISA. xxxv. 8.

> "For evermore the end shall tell
> The unreached Ideal guided well."
> WHITTIER.

A FRIEND described to us lately what it is to make a highway in the East. For two months great forces of men were making preparations. They were laying low and raising up, and the cry was "Prepare, prepare." The last thing done was to sprinkle the surface with yellow sand—the Imperial colour—and then behind the band of horsemen who led the procession, alone on a black mule, rode the young Emperor of China.

In life there are times of sorrow and of suffering, of learning and of discipline, which seem to us like preparing the highway, not only for ourselves but for others; and then there is the easy march, the onward tread of the victorious feet. There are days in our life when the steam-roller beats down the metal stones of disappointment and delay and failure.

These are not joyous days, but grievous; but afterwards there come straight paths for our feet. The very hindrance becomes a help. In our march through life towards our ideal, there are many helps and hindrances. Let us look at some of the hindrances and then at some of the helps. Let us be as earnest as Stanley's followers in the African forest, to resolve as we go on to cut down the high branches, the brushwood and the low undergrowth of creepers. There must be no aimlessness, no putting off.

Surely one great hindrance is want of earnestness and enthusiasm. All around us are in earnest. The followers of the world turn night into day for their avocations and amusements; but have we counted the cost of what it is to be a follower of Christ? Another great hindrance is want of thoroughness. In the matter of our salvation there must be no scamp-work. Another hindrance is surely the "Tyranny of the things seen," the love of and the living in the present. What Tertullian calls "the great interloper sin," that is at the root of all. Paul called out, "O wretched man that I am!" He was struggling after the ideal, but the desire within met the temptation without, and it was only when he looked away to his Ideal, Christ, that he got the victory. A child also felt Paul's struggle. One day among a number of Christmas presents she looked unhappy, and a friend said, "What! not happy with all these; what is wrong?" "Just the old thing that troubles us all:" and the child spelt out in a whisper, S I N. Perhaps the greatest hindrance of all is this want of realisation of the stupendous importance of this life as a preparation for the next. As we sow we shall reap.

One day we left the sides of the Annan and climbed and climbed, passing Ericstane and the "Beef Tub," until we were far away from human habitation, among the moor and the heather. We came to a place whence several streams parted. The dwellers in a lonely cottage could give us little information, but we found that one of the streams was the source of the Tweed. There, in silence among the birds and the clouds, the clear air, and the cool winds, the river sprang, which, as we descended with it, widened and broadened, fed everywhere from lesser streams. Let all our activity for Christ have a source as real and life-giving, even in Him who came to put reality, intensity, nobility into the meanest things of life. He who posts a letter to His glory, instead of letting it lie in his pocket, shall not want call to higher service. For our march through life "we are not promised a chart, but a guide." The nearer we keep to His side the more shall we be helped. Let this be true of our lives—

> "That evermore beside thee on thy way
> The unseen Christ may move,
> That thou may'st lean upon His arm,
> And say, dear Lord, dost Thou approve?"

And talking to Him is just prayer, which is one of our greatest helps. "It is not so much petitioning now as communing," a friend said to us lately. The Hebrew for the word "faithful ones" is "Amen-ers," those who say Amen to His promises and His proposals for their daily life. Prayer is like the sleep of a tired infant. It was cross and fretful, it was hard to get it even into the attitude where it would let its weary head rest, and give itself a chance. It awoke rosy, smiling, satisfied.

> " Lord, what a change within us one short hour
> Spent in Thy presence will prevail to make,
> What heavy burdens from our bosoms take,
> What parchèd grounds refresh, as with a shower!
> We kneel, and all around us seems to lower;
> We rise, and all, the distant and the near,
> Stands forth in sunny outline, brave and clear;
> We kneel how weak, we rise how full of power."

There are various forms of prayer, but this we know that to all of us the call comes, "Pray more, ask more."

Another great help is meditation. In quiet waiting as David did before the Lord, forethought is gained, resolution formed, conscience obeyed, and strength obtained. Linked on to meditation is the food we feed on—the word of God laid bare by His Spirit. What fascination there is in its study in whatever form we take it. And the beauty of all other reading is that it sends us back and back to this living word, which liveth and abideth for ever. The first inspiration, the first start after the ideal, comes in many ways. It may be from the reading of a poem, as with Elizabeth Stuart Phelps, author of the "Gates Ajar," who says of Mrs. Barrett Browning and her poem "Aurora Leigh": "There may be greater poems in our language than ' Aurora Leigh,' but it was many years before it was possible for me to suppose it. . . . I owe to her, distinctly, the first visible aspiration (ambition is too low a word) to do some honest, hard work of my own in the World Beautiful, and for it." It may be from perusal of a book like Law's *Serious Call*, a book "with a strange and moving spiritual pedigree."

We know how Dr. Johnson, George Whitefield, John Wesley, and Thomas Scott spoke of that. It may be from looking at a picture, it may be the inscription on a coffin-lid; but whatever we start from, no progress can be made without feeding on the word by faith. But all these, prayer and meditation, and the word are but the handmaids leading us back again to behold the vision of Him whom having not seen we love.

"When I was young," said Gounod to a friend, "I used to talk of 'I and Mozart.' Later, I said 'Mozart and I'; but now I only say 'Mozart.'"

> "Whom have I in heaven but Thee?
>   And there is none upon earth that I desire beside
>   Thee.
>   My heart and my flesh faileth:
>   But God is the strength of my heart and my portion
>   for ever."

> "Nothing resting in its own completeness
>   Can have worth or beauty: but alone
>   Because it leads and tends to further sweetness,
>   Fuller, higher, deeper than its own.
>   Life is only bright when it proceedeth
>   Towards a truer, deeper life above;
>   Human love is sweetest when it leadeth
>   To a more divine and perfect love."

CHAPTER IV

THE IDEAL OF THE PILGRIM SPIRIT

" Something I may not win attracts me ever—
  Something elusive, yet supremely fair;
Thrills me with gladness, yet contents me never,
  Fills me with sadness, yet forbids despair.

It blossoms just beyond the paths I follow,
  It shines beyond the farthest stars I see;
It echoes faint from ocean caverns hollow,
  And from the land of dreams it beckons me.

It calls, and all my best, with joyful feeling,
  Essays to reach it as I make reply;
I feel its sweetness o'er my spirit stealing,
  Yet know ere I attain it I must die."

"I count all things but loss."—PHIL. iii. 8.
"Confessed that they were pilgrims."—HEB. xi. 13.

IN the former chapters we have been considering the helps and the hindrances to the realisation of our ideal. We shall look in the next two at two ideals realised. We know how with children a blackboard or an object-lesson helps, and is remembered.

Our friend Frances Ridley Havergal left us twenty years ago, but the further we go from the parting with her, and the nearer to the reunion, we see how God did make her an ideal realised, and as such she lives in our hearts and memories. When we revisit her bust in the niche of our heart we cannot help giving God the glory. Under her name and over all her life is written legibly, "Whose I am and whom I serve." The name of the Sculptor shines out everywhere, luminous in the darkness of time, with the light of eternity. Sometimes an artist loves a piece of work which he has so breathed his spirit into as to make it a part of himself, and reserves it for himself. It may be sent awhile to an academy for the inspiration of others, but it is marked with a prohibitive price. We think now, after two decades of years, that this was what God meant by removing Frances Ridley Havergal. "I will that they also be with Me where I am"—with Me where I am in the glory, and with Me where *I am*—as a preacher lately made the word shine with another facet cut on the surface —in the field of service standing beside you. If the air were rarefied enough, if we were more. of spirit and not so held by the flesh, we would know more of

"The mystic sweet communion
With those whose rest is won,"

through Christ the Head. We may think rightly that they are nearer the Head than we are; but one was not very far wrong who said to us recently, "Will you write something on this subject, 'Members of His body; that is, nearer than even brothers and sisters in Christ.'" We throw out the thought, and it may germinate. We think, and think much of the problems of life. Do we think out His designs? Do we add up His sums, of which He keeps the "Answer Book"? Are we tracing the connection between the seed sown by those now at rest and the sheaves of harvest we are helping to bind? There is a mystic communion in service even now between heaven and earth.

About a week ago in our drawing-room the following words were spoken, which seemed as the marriage-service performed between the Keswick movement and the Student Volunteer Missionary one. It seemed the union of the two ideals realised, which we take as our object-lesson. One who has risen up, left all, and followed Christ, said, "What led me to do it was the verse of Miss Havergal's hymn—

> "Take my silver and my gold;
> Not a mite would I withhold.'"

Again, at a meal, the origin of the title of the record of the Liverpool Conference, "Make Jesus King," was discussed, as the proof-sheets were in our house. A flood of thoughts rushed in, and we did not need to think alone of the *title* of her book, *My King*, for, in all her writings, prose and poetry alike, this note of Kingship is found.

In our two object-lessons what strikes us most is the ideal of the pilgrim spirit realised. It is said of our Lord and Master, "There was no room in the inn;" and to speak reverently, when the infant had grown to manhood, He saw the fox dart to its lair, and the bird soar from its nest, and said, "But the Son of Man." We would fain forget it, but the word stands there. As the thought pervades our religious literature, finding exponents in Bunyan and Dante, in our hymns we sing—

> "A pilgrim through this lonely world
> Our blessed Saviour passed."

But is this only to be an ideal life with us? We are sent back to the eleventh of Hebrews to see the ideal realised in the record of the faith and progress of the pilgrims. They "obtained promises." So did our friends now gone home. They believed that what He promised He was able also to perform. The eleventh of Hebrews shows us Abraham and Moses and the Passover night. The Master Himself described the pilgrims' attitude—loins girt, lamp burning, waiting for their Lord. Mr. Radcliffe used to come into his Cannes meetings with the plaid and the alpenstock, because of his delicacy; and they were fit emblems. The mighty spirit was lodged in him in very fragile clay. One who prayed for him and who led, if ever anyone did, the pilgrim life, though she could not be an actual wanderer, had over her porch the words, "Ut migraturus habita." Her loins were ever girt, her lamp ever burning, her daily fare was a Passover meal. All too rare it is to find the pilgrim spirit now. How few send on their treasure before to heaven, leaving little to "will" away of gold or treasure! Without our judging it, folly is seen written on many of the mansions in favourite health resorts. The proprietors outbuild themselves, and have to let to strangers. Or having provided themselves with every new improvement, and for some reason, health or education, having to flit, they could not get a new home because they could not sell the old. In some cases God and Death had been quite left out of the calculation.

Yet very literally is He giving the pilgrim staff and pilgrim heart to some of His chosen. We copied these "Laws of Attainment" from the notebook of a worker who hopes soon to have the ideal of his life realised in India:—

1. The law of reciprocal approach: "Draw nigh to God and He will draw nigh to you."

2. The law of acquisition: "Whatsoever ye ask in prayer, believing, ye shall receive."
3. The law of spiritual accretion and diminution: "To him that hath shall be given . . . from him that hath not shall be taken away even that which he seemeth to have."
4. The law of the only limitation of God: "Your iniquities have separated between you and your God."

His was only one other testimony to the going when the Lord's call is heard, and obedience bringing the perfect freedom of the pilgrim life. In these days the call comes to all, to the individual and to the relatives. Is the mother to accept a foreign merchant's or civilian's hand for her daughter with satisfaction, and refuse to her the joy of being a missionary? The choice, the decision, must be made alone with God. But this we can all have as our ideal, the pilgrim life at home or abroad. We can be ready with our sails set for the first gale of the Spirit. A missionary said to us lately, "When we come back it is the Home Church who should stir us up, and then we would not have to go about speaking." We can open our houses to receive the pilgrims, and be at some trouble to find their whereabouts, for the time of the King's messengers must be spared. When volunteers for the Ashantee War were summoned from the ranks, a whole company stepped forward. Let us send our children to see reviews of troops for our King's great gatherings, such as Liverpool. The schoolboy camps and the Keswick gatherings are the parade-ground. The pilgrim spirit demands that the eye be fixed on the Leader, to receive His marching orders. This loosening from earth will make death a less unwelcome visitor to ourselves and others. For the leasehold of our life is short, and some on foreign shores cannot even have the graves of their dear ones "in perpetuity." The pilgrim spirit demands that the Spirit be not grieved, or our prayers will be like "the dead birds that cannot fly." The pilgrim spirit demands absence of judging or censuring. If we may not too hardly judge those who seem to us willing to remain out of the atmosphere of blessing, neither must the others judge us. "Many will not be lost eternally who will yet be eternal losers." In what measure are we going to have the pilgrim spirit? The spirit of criticism and earthly wisdom may grieve the Holy Spirit. "I thank Thee, O Father, Lord of heaven and earth, that Thou hast hid these things from the wise and prudent, and hast revealed them unto babes. Even so, Father."

We live in a restless age, invention crowding out invention, swift steamers making record crossings, and the eager press rushing to make these records known. But if the two of whom the next chapters speak could return to earth, with what joy would they see the young recruits for our King all over the land offering themselves for His service.

CHAPTER V

AN IDEAL REALISED—

FRANCES RIDLEY HAVERGAL

"I thank Thee for Thy written Word, my God,
    For every sacred line!
But more I thank Thee for Thy humblest saint,
    Whose daily life doth shine—
A living page, most true, most pure, most sweet,
    Fresh from Thy hand divine."

THE spring of 1874 had been cheerless at Bournemouth, with gales, snow-showers, and mist, and we resolved to finish our April holiday at Leamington. Here we found summer, and the warmth in the Jephson gardens was delicious. But springs may go and come, holidays begin and end, with perhaps no deep mark in our hearts or lines in our calendar. This was to be an eventful one, for we found a *friend*.

The friend was Frances Ridley Havergal. She glided like a sunbeam into the garden of our hotel in the street, and gave colour not only to that holiday, but to the three years after, that she remained here. We can still see the slim figure tripping along rather than walking to greet us. We had no common *past*, except the great heritage of pilgrims in a covenant-keeping God; and as our earthly lives had not touched till then, she knew not but that the mourning garb we wore for an aged relative might be for a baby then laughing in his nursery on the Tay, and feared to ask. But we had a common *present*; and she had a newly-found gift from her ascended King to share with us, and told us that the little lemon-coloured booklet entitled *Such a Blessing* was her own history. And we had a common *future*, full of meaning as of mystery. As we heard her story, our barque drifted out to

"Where there was mid-sea and the mighty things."

This note had prepared us for the visit: " I hope to run in and give a short but hearty greeting a little before one o'clock to-morrow. The day after, I have an entirely free-afternoon. You must not call on me. Christians need never stand on ceremony; we understand each other too well, and those who love the Lord Jesus Christ are never mere acquaintances, much less strangers, but always friends."

Her eager spirit got up a meeting in an incredibly short time to hear about Mr. Moody's Edinburgh work. We had many discussions about the blessing she had received, and which it was the fashion then to speak of as *it*. She maintained that *it* was something to be received during the Christian life, whilst we argued that many children of God received *it* at conversion.

In a note from Switzerland, written in the same autumn, there was the beautiful blending of evangelistic effort and deepening knowledge. "God has tried our faith about Leamington. There is terrible unbelief, and the town is afraid to wet its respectable feet in any wave of blessing. But in *His* time the answer will come, and then you will rejoice with us. *Now* I understand why Dr. S. found nothing new in R. P. S.'s teachings. He told me he had been under Dr. Candlish's ministry, so no wonder; for that splendid book of his on the First Epistle of St. John is just '*it.*' But we have not had that teaching in England, and I understand now why I was told that Dr. Candlish was 'not sound.' You see you in Scotland have been ahead of us."

And again:

"Though we 'know' that our 'labour is not in vain in the Lord,' it is very nice to have pleasant proofs of it. And I would, perhaps, rather say 'suffering' than 'labour.' For there is no 'labour' in writing hymns or poems, but there is often long and deep 'suffering,' which goes to the making of what is written in a few minutes. I could not have written 'Disappointment' had I not known and experienced it, and if I had not thus known it, that little drop of comfort could not have reached you. So it is delightfully true that 'none of us liveth to himself' in this sense; and while there is most sweet rest in such personal comfort as 'whom the Lord loveth He chasteneth,' it has long seemed to me a higher and more blessed thing to feel that the trials He sends are not for ourselves alone, but for others' sake and for His work's sake. 'Unto you it is given . . . to suffer for His sake.' Does it not make suffering lighter to feel that it is somehow (no matter about our seeing how) for His glory, that by it He is making us more 'meet for the Master's use'? And that not only here, but it may be for unguessed glorious service millions of years to come, when 'His servants shall serve Him,' and oh so joyfully and perfectly! May I give you another thought which has helped me over some trials, namely, that every separate trial shall have its own blessed 'nevertheless, afterward.' This struck me strongly a year or two ago, and has been a curiously practical help to me, for every trial now sets me hoping and wondering what 'afterward' of 'peaceful fruit' is my Father going to cause this trial to yield? And so I keep looking forward, and vividly expecting some special blessing, near or remote, to follow every separate trial, believing that however unseen at present, it is surely linked with it in God's purpose. I am so burdened with correspondence and work that it is very rarely I can indulge in such a long letter, but I have written to you as a sort of little treat to myself."

Another letter runs thus:

"PYRMONT VILLA, LEAMINGTON.

"I wonder *why?* But we never have a 'why' without the Lord's having a full 'because,' whether He sees it well to tell it or not to us. So there must be a 'because' in this seeming denial to our prayer. *Is* it an answer that now in this matter it is *definitely* given to her to suffer for His sake? May she have all the sweetness and hidden blessedness of that gift and a special and gracious 'nevertheless *afterwards*' as well! I have just heard that a French Wesleyan pastor in the south of France has been so roused by *Such a Blessing* to seek *more* for himself, that he too has got 'such a blessing,' and has gone among his people with new power, and God has used him already for the conversion of many members of his flock and the quickening of others. Isn't that nice? What shall I send you? 'What He hath promised, He is able also to perform.'"

"THE MUMBLES, SWANSEA, *October* 24.

"It is worth knowing something of under-the-surface sorrows, if one may thereby have the privilege of bringing a drop of God's comfort to others—the same comfort, and yet each has such different sorrows. I have just begun an entirely new life-era. Since my poor mother's death, last May, our old home has been finally broken up and furniture sold, and now my very dear elder sister and I have just settled into lodgings here for the winter, partly for economy, partly to be well out of reach, as both of us were very worn and weary, and sorely needing rest and quiet. I think this is likely to be a permanent arrangement,—at anyrate this address will always find me.

"All the 'changes and chances of this mortal life' seem to bring one into view of fresh promises; don't you find it so too? There are so many which one can't get the full preciousness of till one is brought into some specially corresponding position of need or sorrow; and as one after another lights up, one wonders, What next?"

This was to be our last note from her pen. "What next?" As the pilgrim mused and wondered, she all at once sighted the Golden Gate. Her life was a true poem. It had kept pace with her prayers. "A great deal of living must go to very little writing," she used to say. She walked with God, and was not, for God took her. The mist that came up from the sea, as she took the temperance pledges of the donkey-boys on their saddles, was the descending of the cloud that was to part her from our sight. And now, all over the land, organs peal out—

"Take my life, and let it be
Consecrated, Lord, to Thee;"

and as we catch the echoes, we look round to see the fulfilment of her prayer. On the mountains at home and abroad the feet of well-tried messengers are swift and beautiful; the silver and the gold fall into the treasuries; literature increases presenting the aspect of truth in which she loved to sun herself; and, best of all, the young press forward to offer themselves willingly as recruits for our great Captain.

> " For slowly as the years go on,
> With thankfulness we find
> That Death, which takes so much away,
> Has left so much behind;
> The light which glorified our past
> In blessing lingers yet,
> And lessons learned from holy lives
> More deep with years shall get."

CHAPTER VI

AN IDEAL REALISED—

REGINALD RADCLIFFE

> " To me fair memories belong
> Of scenes that used to bless,
> For no regret, but present song
> And lasting thankfulness;
> And very soon to break away,
> Like types, in fairer things than they."

THERE is another who to us lived an ideal life, was an ideal realised, who went home in the close of 1895. Almost for twenty years he was allowed to live on after the sweet singer went home. She did not live to see the " Keswick " movement grow and spread, but she tuned up the orchestra. He did not live to see the conference in his dear Liverpool, but the prophetic soul saw from his Pisgah that promised land of conquest.

When we read in the columns of the *Daily Chronicle* that Reginald Radcliffe had gone home, and when, some weeks later, we got in the opening days of the year thrilling accounts of the Students' International Missionary Conference at Liverpool, the above lines seemed true. We looked back at some of our old journals after there came to us from Liverpool such sentences as these: " It is a wonderful convention. I wish all our children were in it. This is the work for men to do who mean to be men at all. All the rest is like children pulling crackers." . . . " I had read the *Spectator* article on Noah; but this modern miracle of a thousand missionary conferents beats the Flood. These are the men and women who *have* the future."

The " fair memories " of Reginald Radcliffe are very distinct, and we stand in transition years, for surely fairer things are coming. He is already among the fairer things, and his passing away has caused a strange blending of *then* and *now*. When asked by us to write a motto in a book, he wrote the one word " Nigh." It was the keynote of his life.

The first sight of him we had was at Perth in 1860. We played in an attic room at Springland with the stranger children who had come from Liverpool, and whose missionary names Brainerd and Heber remained with us. When the older people had gone to an evening meeting we were left together. Outside was the quiet flowing Tay, and beyond, the trains rushing to Dunkeld which called us often to the window. There was the railway, the river, and the road running side by side as they do so often in our Scottish straths and passes. Below was the tower on the river's brink, where Mr. Radcliffe loved to be alone with God. We remember taking our place with our mother and grandmother on the day in August of the great open-air gathering, on the raised wooden seats on the South Inch, and well remember the giving out of the psalm—

> " O God, what time Thou didst go forth
> Before Thy people's face ; "

and the power of the addresses by Radcliffe and others. What struck the child-mind was that there stood a man who, when he prayed, believed in God, and got what he asked, and saw the Spirit descend. He asked the anxious to adjourn to Free St. Leonard's, which scores of men did, while the women went into a tent near. Week after week for many nights after, we helped our grandmother in the work in the side-room, as she could not overtake the many seeking help. The power of the Lord was present to heal, and the talk between the evangelist and his hostess going home in the cab was like chapters of the Acts lived over again.

Some ten years later, our father engaged rooms in the hotel at Cannes for Mr. Radcliffe. To the proprietor and his visitors, the *salon* was just a number on a floor ; to those who heard it given out at the meetings which he soon began to hold, it was to be a trysting-place for heaven. To the girl of eighteen there again came the vision of the ideal realised—a worm threshing mountains. He had faith in God, and God did not disappoint him. The meetings for the working men in the "Gymnase Médicale" are those which we remember most distinctly. The excursions of that winter are dim, the friendships then formed are mostly severed, but the power of God seen and known remains a part of the Eternal within us. The printing of the bills, the practising of the choir, the old hymns that had a new zest in French dress, the little meetings for prayer, the blue blouses of the French *ouvriers*, and the walk home in dark nights over muddy fields, now all built over by hotels, are all memories, but the personality of the man and the presentness of his God are the most vivid. We think we hear him say what we noted at the time:—

"Dear friends, I am here like yourselves seeking health. I have been asked to hold one or two meetings in this place. I feel a great desire to do something for the dear people around us. I invite your help. For this we shall all best gèt strength, and be prepared, by forgetting for the moment that there are any souls to save, forgetting the gospel, and looking to ourselves. God does not wish us to remain babes, He wants full-grown men. He will not have stunted believers, He will not have us to be always as little children; He wants men, men full-grown, men and women filled with the Holy Ghost. He did not send His twelve children forth, but bade them *wait* for the promise, till the power came. The power did come, but not at once; there was the tension of faith, the drawing out of desires, the realising of helplessness, and the being shut up to God. And then the power came down; and so with us here, the blessing must begin with ourselves. And when the Spirit comes to the instrument or place, then, as a matter of course, the dead awake, one word is dropped here, and another there, and then the careless man awakes, the wicked one turns. I beg of you all to spend the time between this and Thursday morning in prayer, wrestling with God. 'Ask, and ye shall receive.' You must get the thing before you leave your knees. God is well able to move Cannes from this little room without anything being done."

After two prayers in French, Mr. Radcliffe gave out for us to read Psalm cxxvi., and asked it to be read in French. Mr. Radcliffe said: "We shall take this Psalm as the motto of our work in Cannes, and expect to see it made good. 'When the Lord'— 'When the Lord'— better stop here for to-day. There's enough here to fill our minds in these three words, 'When the *Lord*' . . . not Samson, David, or any man, not the pastor or evangelist, not believers, but '*When the Lord.*' Let us stop here and all get in, completely hidden, behind the Lord. This Conqueror never lost a battle, this Promiser never broke His word. This Captain goes first, does all, and bids His poor people follow Him. Does He want to do a mighty work like to the tunnelling of a great mountain? He does not take an axe, a spear, or even a staff, does not call for gunpowder, but picks up a worm—a poor grub—a small worm such as goes into the chrysalis—and with it He tunnels Mont Cenis. 'Fear not, worm Jacob, thou shalt thresh mountains.' The Lord goeth before. We are worms in His hand. God's invariable rule is still as Christ laid it down, 'According to your faith be it unto you.' Oh that He would begin here to teach these worm-like children of His to be talking to the mountains in faith, and bidding them go down into the Mediterranean there. We must wrestle on in prayer till all the barriers and hills that oppose His work in Cannes be cast into the Mediterranean. Before we shall have done with this Psalm, in Cannes shall we not be as men that dreamed? We shall be saying, 'What opening graves are these?' 'Wasn't that man dead?' 'Is *that* woman praising Him?' 'They that sow in tears *shall*' (and that's the right tense of the verb) 'reap in joy'—shall doubtless, beyond all doubt, 'come again rejoicing.'

"I would fain go to all the *table d'hôtes* in Cannes and preach Jesus, if I had only strength. I would fain go from one drawing-room to another, and if one person in Cannes won't receive the message, then go on to another place; and if one person on this side of the bay won't receive the word, then go to some one on the other. The evangelist's commission is to go to every creature."

Then there were some more prayers in French and English, and Mr. Radcliffe gave out "*Tel que je suis*" ("Just as I am"), the same tune and our words translated. Mr. Radcliffe asked any who might not be quite sure that they had Jesus, to remain. Afterwards he had conversation with some who were already anxious at that meeting.

In the autumn of 1884 we slept for a night under the same roof with him in Copenhagen, and did not know till he had gone. He was at his old work, on the old errand, but we only saw the name posted up as we passed out for our drive next day. So near and yet so far may friends often be in these great hotels!

In December of that year he came to Edinburgh, bringing Stanley Smith and Studd to address our students, and so to begin the movement in our university which has borne such wonderful fruit. Here was the Scottish fountain-head of the Liverpool Convention. A year later he was again with us, among his companions being two other Cambridge students, one of whom wrote his address in the visitors' book as "Corpus Christi College, Cambridge," and the other, "China Inland Mission, Shanghai."

And did not the Lord let him slay more in death than even in life, when hardly had he left us, ere there was held in his own city the greatest student conference on missions that has ever been seen? In our quiet harbour the great waves have come as from the broad Atlantic, and we feel as if we must slip our moorings and put out to sea, lest we or any near to us miss the meaning of this tide of blessing.

CHAPTER VII

THE QUEST OF THE IDEAL—

IN MEMORY

"I will set no base thing before mine eyes."
Ps. ci. 3 (R.V.).

"None sends his arrow to the mark in view,
Whose hand is feeble, or his aim untrue."
COWPER.

As in the photograph of the woman wearily toiling up the five stone steps, so our daily life is often the upward monotonous climb, even though we have the light beyond. We shall perhaps in the few practical chapters to follow, find, as the old woman did, the steps irksome at the time but pleasant in the retrospect. For the little things make the big things easy. As one has said, " Between the big things we are afraid are too high for us to do, and the little things which we think beneath our doing, the risk is that we shall end in doing nothing." We cannot all climb heights, but to us all there is the staircase of daily life. We like this picture because we feel that for the old woman, too, there was an ideal and a goal. We shall be well rewarded if the steps in the following chapters make the lives of any go more smoothly, by removing hindrances, and filling them with hope.

As steps cut in the ice, as a track in the desert, as a path on the mountain-side, we give in this and the following chapters some hints to help travellers who have started.

How important in any undertaking is forethought! Minutes well spent now may save hours after. What should we take and what should we let go in life's journey? Miss Havergal says that in climbing she gave up nearly all, little by little, till, instead of her " Practical Guide," she only carried the few pages cut out necessary for that day's excursion.

It is told of Jenny Lind that she said: " Memory, I engaged thee to be my servant, and thou hast not failed me." Thomas Fuller says: " Memory will easily preserve matter well arranged, just as one will carry twice more weight trussed and packed up in bundles, than when it lies untowardly flapping and hanging around his shoulders." We owe much to the training of one whose business habits left a lasting impression on us. Our father took great pains with us. We were sent to the dictionary to hunt up words for ourselves, or to the directory to learn the rates of postage, instead of being told. We were warned not to commence our letters with apologies; always to acknowledge money on receipt; to be specially careful of the property of other people, and never to keep books long on loan. The pamphlet which we thought we had put up carefully was held up by the ends of the wrapper, and let fall out, to show that we were slovenly; and we were told how people disliked a letter misplaced or missing in their names. We were made to carry a pencil and notebook to aid our memory. But best of all, there was the living, consistent example before us, the embodiment of business habits putting us to shame. Now, after thirty years, as the pattern of a carpet, or piece of willow-pattern china makes some old memory live again, so some line in a book or sentence in a sermon makes his maxims speak once more.

In this restless age much fret and worry would be spared if the young early acquired business habits. Christ said: "He that is faithful in a very little is faithful also in much." The girl who practises faithfully on the schoolroom piano till the hour strikes, will not fail when called to play her part in the orchestra of life. We see daily in a household how much time and temper might be saved by simply having memory in little things. If we drift with the tide, and let things slip, we are great losers, more than we shall ever know. An idea comes, a thought presses in, but we put it off, and it never is embodied in action. The windows of our mind get swollen through damp, and will not open; and so new ideas, like fresh air, cannot come in. The stop-cocks of memory will not work through want of use.

> "It's the stream swiftly flowing that keeps aff the frost,
> And the friction that keeps aff the rust, man;
> And they gather aye weel wha let naething be lost,
> And the rest leave tae Heaven in trust, man."

It is the busy, active workers who never refuse us help; the idle ones are always "too busy to have time." If we simply answer a letter by return of post, our friend can plan a whole week of arrangements with comfort. When a letter comes too late, we feel as if we paid double postage for the delay. We suffer waste of brain tissue wondering when the answer will come, and dissatisfaction when it has come. "He gives twice who gives quickly" is true of much more than money. If one person is put out of temper, he in his turn depresses others, and so on and on.

One friend was so very punctual in taking his seat in the railway carriage that a child, his companion, was in constant terror that she would be left alone. This was excessive, and there is danger in too much attention to trivialities and details, but hardly in those things which concern a household's comfort. Different natures and dispositions will always cause each other some amount of discomfort, as in the case of the horse and the ox ploughing together. There are trains like the German Bummelzug, which stop at all the stations and march slowly, but may carry much precious freight. It would not do if all were expresses. The percentage of collisions would increase.

But "memory without judgment is like a treasure-house without treasure." Some have had to listen patiently to long conversations, and learn to be politely silent, when perhaps the information they were longing to convey would have been to the persistent talker great gain. We educate each other by enforced silences. We are almost touching a vein of gold when a conversation has to be broken off—a visitor is announced. But if we cultivate prompt and kindly thoughtfulness, the mind will get so agile and tractable that it will make use even of interruptions to diffuse happiness, and make our friends feel more at ease. What a purifying of the air there is in even five minutes of healthy reading aloud! The minutes are long and drawn out, and the mud of a troubled pool goes to the bottom. Perhaps conscience rings her alarum-bell, and a message from the shore of eternity meets us on this "brief wave of life." Even looking silently into a clock's face gives us time to hear the tick of these lines as the pendulum seems to say—

"Improve time in time while time doth last,
For all time is no time when time is past."

Anyhow, more reading and less talking would leave fewer regrets at the day's end, and if conversation followed, it would be fuller in tone and richer in flavour. Many look back to George Macdonald's reading aloud of some poem on his "at-home" day in Bordighera, as a jewel in the bright setting of the blue Mediterranean and the grey olive. Quiet thought and planning for a week or a month beforehand is like laying smooth rails for the days to glide along. There are a number of relations, all of the same clan, for they have fallen in love with each other and intermarried — Memory, Promptitude, Method, Order, Neatness, and more distant cousins whom we do not take time to name. They whisper to each other what a saving it is when a collector's money is left out on the slab, and a shop parcel that has to be returned is awaiting the messenger. To the young, stairs do not count for much. A long sleep, not some broken sleeps, makes each day's simple living a delight. You are now hopeful, fresh and vigorous, and life lies like an unsolved conundrum, of which the experience of later life holds the key. You have what a writer has called "enthusiasm resembling a cloak of three pile to keep its gloss in wear" during the friction of years.

You think you have an unlimited supply of time before you. In later years you may find you are in debt. "For who knows most, him loss of time most grieves." Knowing the value of time, let us use it judiciously. Knowledge and diligence! We feel, like Peter, that we can hardly separate them. The words are like a pair of eyes or ears or hands. They work together, and are not yet jealous of each other.

> "Rest is not quitting
> The busy career;
> Rest is the fitting
> Of self to its sphere.
>
> 'Tis loving and serving
> The highest and best!
> 'Tis onwards, unswerving,—
> And that is true rest."

CHAPTER VIII

THE QUEST OF THE IDEAL—

IN MONEY

" The Master commits five talents to the servant, and the trust is shrewdly managed. The five becomes ten, and the Master is fully satisfied. What reward does He propose for His servant? Is it release from labour and responsibility—a future in contrast with the past? Is it, so to say, retirement and a pension? It would not be absurd, but it would be less than the best. The past shapes the future; and this servant, having served his apprenticeship, becomes himself a master, 'ruler over many things.'"

IT is remarked, " In the Bible there has been more said about money, the use of it, the abuse of it, the curse of it, and the blessing of it, than on the doctrine of justification by faith." As long as we are in this world we shall have to do with money; we cannot get away from it. When we go to a new country, one of the first things we do is to seek a good exchange, and to learn the coins. A missionary thus writes of the Chinese: " Wherever people are met, cash is almost invariably the subject of discourse. They talk cash, they think cash, they live cash. Some of the most amusing stories for children treat on the subject of cash; it is said that three-fifths of all the proverbs in the Chinese language have seen the light first through the small square hole in the centre of a cash."

Where there are no coins, the missionary and the merchant carry with them the calico or the beads for which they get goods in exchange. There is always, all the same, the giving and the receiving, and in the East, the weary bargaining. Our children copy us, and in counters or copper or paper pence transact their business. It would be an interesting study to note down the passages all through our Bible bearing on this subject. We have the warnings of Achan and Gehazi, of Ananias and Sapphira, the tragic end of Judas, and the last glimpse of Demas. Christ says: " How hardly shall they that have riches enter the kingdom;" and yet the same voice says: " Shew me a penny; render unto Cæsar the things that are Cæsar's, and unto God the things that are God's." He gave to all their due, and from the paths of the sea, in the fish's mouth, His tribute-money came. Matthew and Zaccheus were both His willing followers, Who for our sakes " became poor." Paul soars very high in his resurrection chapter, and closes with the verse which seems to bridge the chasm, and link on the highest to the commonest, the heavenly to the earthly. " Wherefore, my beloved brethren, be ye steadfast, unmovable. . . . Now concerning the collection." It seems as if this verse were a place of repair for tired collectors down to this very day. But why should collecting money for Christ's kingdom be weary work? If each application for money were answered by return of post, or at least the same day, how much time would be saved. One collector told us how she wrote twice for a small sum of money, got no reply, and at last advanced the money on trust, resolving if she did not receive it to give it herself, as the card had to be given in. A minister said there were three things needed in collectors: " Intelligence, promptitude, and enthusiasm;" and the literal reading of a familiar verse is, "God loveth an hilarious giver." But how many are eager to gain and slow to give, and so miss great joy! It is best when a certain proportion can be set apart consecrated to the Lord. Where our treasure is there our heart is also; so let us with joy send our treasure where it will reap great return in His treasury. That is a sure investment, with no liabilities, but with the highest interest. "Riches do not *take* to themselves wings, they *make* to themselves wings;" but what we give to Christ is returned into our own bosom a hundredfold.

In all dealings with money there should be exact accounts kept, and all accounts paid with no delay; and our children should be taught to do this early. There is a strange "deceitfulness" about riches, and "the love of money is the root of all evil." About this very thing Peter said to Ananias, "Why hath Satan filled thy heart to lie to the Holy Ghost?" Marcus Antoninus said: "Such as are thy habitual thoughts, such will be the character of thy mind; for the soul is dyed by the thoughts." How many hearts are withered to the core through gold, yellow as an autumn leaf. Some are even more than withered; they are killed by what they prided themselves in, as in the story of the old miser. "He had caused a cellar to be constructed with an iron door and a complicated iron lock, of which he only knew the secret. In his cellar he heaped up his treasure—metallic treasure—which he loved to handle, the rattle of it sounding as the most harmonious music in his ears. One day when he and his wealth were *tête-à-tête*, the door shut upon them. It was some time before the man was missed, and then it took time to find the workman who had made the mysterious lock. When at last he came the cellar was a sepulchre. He who lay there in the deformity of a last convulsion had been dead for several days."

It is better to give than to lend, for lending often separates friends, and is bad for the borrowers. " Hoping for nothing again " is one of Christ's maxims; but when we give to Him we draw interest at once. How much thought is given about investments, some even wishing to live on the interest of their interests; and we hear how small a return is got for money because it is so plentiful. Christ's kingdom is not only safe, but the return is unvarying. God is our Judge. He looketh on the heart, and knows what is withheld as well as given. This we know, that the joy of those who have given in their lifetime has been immense in seeing the fruit of their giving, and this liberal spirit is infectious. It has been our privilege to know one of the largest annual contributors to the student movement in America and mission lands. Through others we heard that she supports thirty or forty foreign and native missionaries. The natural result followed that this friend wanted to visit the mission stations herself, and went. When Christians of leisure and means are planning a winter's tour abroad, it gives great zest to combine in the search for health a visit to scenes of missionary labour, as the merchant goes to see the increase of his ground in foreign plantations. We have said that this giving is infectious, but we feel we cannot do better than quote from a letter of Mr. L. D. Wishard, Treasurer of the World's Student Christian Federation. He had told us of an old woman who each night baked her bread which she sold by day, all the time praying earnestly in her prayer for foreign missionaries. We asked to know more, and this was the reply—

"The most interesting case of liberality that has ever come to my notice was that of the 'old bread-woman,' as you characterise her. Among the first contributions which came for Mr. M'Conaughy's work in India was one of five pounds from an unknown lady in one of our Western towns. I, supposing that a giver of that amount had still another five pound contribution to dispose of, wrote her over a year ago for a similar contribution for the extension of our work in Asia. The substance of her reply was as follows: 'How deeply I regret that I cannot give you another five pounds. If I had the money, Mr. M'Conaughy would not have to wait long for the building which he is trying to secure as headquarters for this movement in India. I am, however, an old woman in my sixty-seventh year, and am dependent upon my own exertions for my support. I had been saving something with which to provide for my wants in my old age; but when the call came for help for this student movement in India, I could not resist the desire to have a part in it, for I can think of no more important work in the world than this student movement. I, therefore, sent you five pounds, which represented the savings of an entire winter. I cannot give you five pounds now, but I must give two pounds more. I pray for you and Mr. M'Conaughy three times every day. At midnight when I get up to mix my bread I make you and your work my special subject of prayer.' I afterwards learned that she had been for some time dependent upon her bread-making for a living, and my informant told me that there was no more inspiring sight than the face of that old woman as she moved about the streets in her old-fashioned bonnet and faded dress, with a large basket of bread on her arm, her face shining like the face of Moses after his long interview with God. The recital of this incident has already influenced some large gifts for the student work. In one single day the salary of one of our men was pledged, chiefly, I believe, because of the impression made by hearing the letter from this old lady, Margaretta Moses."

Let us enter a room in the gay city of Paris. The deceased countess was found dead in her chair by her *concierge*, and on her knees was resting a box containing gold, while near her was another receptacle containing bonds and securities amounting in value to £800. "Lay not up for yourselves treasures upon the earth . . . but lay up for yourselves treasures in heaven." Another incident we cull, not from the basket of the poor bread-woman, but from the collection plate of a city church. It shows how the liberal heart deviseth liberal things, and is inventive in its giving. Some diamonds were found in a box among the coins. They were redeemed by the chairman, and set by him in a brooch for the wife of the missionary who had been speaking, whose health obliged her to remain at home.

As in individual life, so with great gatherings. The presence of God's Spirit was wondrously felt at the Students' Liverpool Conference last January ; and as a natural result, as at Pentecost the money was laid at the apostles' feet, as for the tabernacle the people offered willingly, so the money poured in. A friend writes thus : " After some speeches on the movement as a whole, and on missions and stewardship of money, Mr. Sherwood Eddy gave one of those brief, rare speeches that come with the power of the Spirit of God, and move hearts far more deeply than the mere words could do, and during silent prayer promissory slips were handed round. £1500 were needed by the movement, and £1630 were raised in ten minutes that night, without the faintest approach to begging. As a result, not only has the Conference been paid for and the year's work financed, but the movement has been started on the Continent for the first time, an advance that will mean more than we can measure." One Cambridge student wrote: "£250 and myself besides." It was a wonderful forecast of the millennium, as it was a repetition of Pentecost. The ideal will be real when the greatest impediments of some shall become the greatest power in the service of Christ, because stamped with His superscription. What is to some a dead-weight dragging them down shall then be as dynamite to blast the mountains. Each in our measure can hasten on the day.

We heard a friend speculating on what would become of all the " capital " at the Day of Judgment. To some who have been at Liverpool, it was as if God had cleansed what they called common in this very matter of money. When a student was studying with one candle instead of two, and a companion coming in asked what he meant, he said, "The evangelisation of the world in our generation."

> "'All very well, but the good Lord Jesus
> has had His day.'
> 'Had? Has it come? It has only dawn'd.
> It will come by and by.'"

CHAPTER IX

THE QUEST OF THE IDEAL—

IN TIME

> " Seek not earth's prizes;
> Whoso wise is,
> Tests them by a dying hour
> For things you get not, long not, fret not,
> Ruled by duty's power.
>
> When harvest beckons, who that reckons
> Worth of moments, wants to play?
> Awake immortals! heaven's bright portals
> Open stand to-day.
> My soul, take care; use well thy share
> Of time so costly and so rare.
> Hast thou a mind a home to find?
> 'Tis now thou must prepare."

WE have seen at a children's gathering how eagerly some would crumble a piece of cake in search of the ring, thimble, or sixpence, till they found one of their treasures. To some minds the fascination is great of taking words to pieces, breaking them up, finding the root, and seeing the "visual image" before them. The French for the word "now" seems so much better than ours—"*maintenant*"—what your hand grasps at the moment. We must redeem the time, buy up the opportunity. The Auctioneer—Life, with his assistant—Circumstance, holds out the precious ware we call time, the moment, "*le maintenant.*" Shall our ideal be to make what the hand holds, but must soon drop, worth having for ever? How much would be gained if all the odd minutes were bought up. The chances are, that if we do not do a thing at the moment, we shall never do it at all. Lady Nairne's sister employed the minutes that elapsed between the ringing of the gong for dinner and the arriving of the guests, in embroidering a table-cover. Sir James Simpson had to wait for a steamer at Burntisland, and he spent the time making experiments on the eels with chloroform. One day, not long ago, we are told, Mr. Gladstone was going a drive into Chester after luncheon. His pudding was very hot, so he went away from the table, changed his clothes, got ready for the drive, and came back and ate his pudding, thus using the minutes it took to cool. When the luncheon gong sounds he lays down his pen, and is first in the dining-room. Promptitude generally goes along with time-saving habits. When a duty comes to us, let it be done at once, and the time thus saved seems to go into the bank with the thing done, as immediate interest at once.

One other way of saving time is, concentration, that is, the art of giving undivided attention to the thing of the moment. A student from America called on us, but left no address on his card. We had no clue to his whereabouts, and had to write to Philadelphia for the address. Older people are sometimes to blame in not giving express utterance as to their wishes, and time is saved when an exact pattern accompanies an order. When visiting a family we noticed that the older and more retired member saved the time of the younger. It was like a General Post Office, where letters collected from all the pillar-boxes were sorted: the best news were gathered and sifted, and spread abroad among the children. Or, to change the illustration, it seemed like a junction of a great railway line, where trains were made up and started to the minute. Dr. Welldon's three rules for teachers were: "Answer letters; Make up your minds; Keep appointments." Certainly indecision is a fruitful source of loss of time.

> " It isn't the thing you do, dear,
>   It's the thing you leave undone,
>   Which gives you a bit of heartache
>   At the setting of the sun.
>   The tender word forgotten,
>   The letter you did not write,
>   The flower you might have sent, dear
>   Are your haunting ghosts to-night.
>
>   The stone you might have lifted
>   Out of another's way,
>   A bit of heartsome counsel,
>   You were hurried too much to say;
>   The loving touch of the hand, dear,
>   The gentle winsome tone,
>   That you had no time nor thought for,
>   With troubles enough of your own."

An experience we had in August last left a deep impress on our minds, both as to the uncertainty and the preciousness of time. The Highland train was advancing at half speed into the Newtonmore station. We had just looked out at a hill, on whose side there was a white patch of snow. Then a thud, —a collision. "Will another shock come? Is this all?" At that moment all along the train strange experiences were lived through. Professor Dobie was taken, and his favourite horse beside him was spared. One minister was looking at the view, when the window was smashed. Another passenger undoing wraps got a most hurtful twist. During the two hours of waiting in the rain among the sufferers one realised how short one's working day may be,—how soon the night may come.

This moment, this day may be the last in the place of opportunity.

> " The period of life is brief;
> It is the red in the red rose leaf,
> It is the gold in the sunset sky,
> It is the flight of a bird on high;
> But one may fill the space
> With such an infinite grace,
> That the red shall vein all time,
> And the gold through the ages shine,
> And the bird fly swift and straight
> To the portals of God's own gate."

We sometimes wish that we had five quarters in the hour, and also extra hands and extra feet. It is best to employ well what we have. "Our possessions are in heaven; therefore, sons of men, purchase unto yourselves by these transitory things which are not yours, what is yours, and shall not pass away." We may grudge that so much time must be spent, and thought given to these transitory things; but this is our training-school for the great future.

One great saving of time is gained by putting away

a thing when we are done with it, and then there is no searching when we need it again. "Disorder," says Xenophon, "seems to me something like as if an husbandman should throw into his granary barley and wheat and peas together, and then, when he wants barley bread or wheaten bread or peas, should have to abstract them grain by grain, instead of having them separately laid up for use." Is there not for us, even in common things, a lesson from what the apostles saw in the empty Easter tomb, in the linen clothes lying, and the napkin that was about His head wrapped together in a place by itself?

Forethought is another secret of saving time. It removes impediments, and prepares the way. "It is," as Frances Willard says, "doing good according to a plan." But it needs forethought and precision or business habits at both ends, else the scheme miscarries. If every order came home executed as it was ordered, what a saving of time and worry there would be. We must learn to think. "Whatsoever thy hand findeth to do, do it with thy might."

"Lange Leben ist nicht viel Leben:
Viel wirken ist viel Leben."

And even at the very end the word will be true of us which is written on Green the historian's grave at Mentone, "He died learning."

We all know by our failures where the leakage has been. Whether we have let our "senses make a playground of our mind by folly," or held too many "debating societies in our cerebrum" by indecision, we can now make a fresh start after our ideal, and resolve to make the most of each moment as it flies.

Let us utilise every power we possess for Christ and His service. Let us see that our feet are not tripped up in the threadbare gossip of the hour. Let us provoke to love and good works, and organise frequent prayer-meetings to increase the love of prayer. Prayer will give us messages to others, and teach us to take the initiative for Him. Dr. Gordon, Boston, tells how the most useful man in one of their churches was converted through the word of a Christian lady, spoken across the counter when he was selling goods to her. One dear servant of Christ, now at rest, said he got great opportunities to testify for Christ when the hairdressers were cutting his hair. Another aged worker, living alone in the country, never let a message-girl leave without a word said, or a book or orange given. These faithful servants fulfilled Paul's injunction to the believers, both at Ephesus and Colosse, to buy up their opportunities. We shall never lack calls to more earnestness. Even as we write, a prince, a painter, a musician have all been called away.

There is a power which is sometimes stronger even than the realisation of the importance and the fleetingness of time. We are told that the seven years that Jacob worked for Rachel seemed like a day, for the love he had to her. Love makes havoc of time and distance. Faith may be the lantern which throws on the screen of our heart the vision that allures us to make much of time in pursuing our ideal; but Love is the operator, Faith worketh by Love. When we feel that the personal living Christ is the motive-power of our life, the mainspring of every action, then alone does the importance of the *maintenant* come in, to live and use the moment for Him ; for, as the lines say—

> " The loss of Gold is much,
> The loss of Time is more,
> But the loss of Jesus Christ is such
> As no man can restore."

CHAPTER X

THE QUEST OF THE IDEAL—

IN BOOKS

"Let us thank God for books. When I consider what some books have done for the world, and what they are doing; how they keep up our hope, awaken new courage and faith, soothe pain, give an ideal life to those whose homes are hard and cold, bind together distant ages and foreign lands, create new worlds of beauty, bring down truths from heaven,—I give eternal blessings for this gift, and pray that we may use it aright, and abuse it not."—JAMES FREEMAN CLARKE.

IT was our privilege to hear Thomas Carlyle deliver his rectorial address in the Music Hall in 1866. He then divided books into two classes when he said, " I conceive that books are like men's souls, divided into sheep and goats. Some few are going up, and carrying us up, heavenward; calculated, I mean, to be of priceless advantage in teaching,—in forwarding the teaching of all generations. Others, a frightful multitude, are going down, down ; doing ever the more and the wider and the wilder mischief. Keep a strict eye on that latter class of books, my young friends ! "

We remember during a course of Astronomical Lectures given in our school days going at night out

on a country road to study the stars. The eager
eyes might have spent the time gazing up and
scanning the heavens. It was more profitable to
fix the eye with the help of the telescope on one
constellation or one planet, on the Plough, or on
Mars or Jupiter. We would like to speak of one or
two helpful books, not for connoisseurs in this de-
partment, but for those who are making out their first
list or catalogue, their first skeleton map of an unknown country. Emerson says: " Private readers
. . . would serve us by leaving each the shortest note
of what he found. . . . Each shall give us his grains
of gold, after the washing." We got these grains of
gold in the following letter, when we asked for a
course of reading-aloud in a country house by the
sea :—

"I should say, read M'Crie's *Life of Knox*, or
M'Crie's (the younger) *Sketches of Scottish Church
History*, or Stanley's *Jewish Church*, or his *Life of
Arnold*, or *Memorials of a Quiet Life*, or Hugh Miller's
My Schools and Schoolmasters, or Trevelyan's
Macaulay, or Farrar's *Paul*. Perhaps the last or first
two would be best ; only get one, get it done. Before
you begin each evening's reading, get your reader to
question you upon last day's lesson. That is worth
two readings. History is the very best kind of reading. It connects, collects, and cools one's mind. It
gives you illustrations, examples that light up your
own life and the life of the present day. Religious
history is perhaps the best for us; but there is no
good history of Scotch or English religion. If you
take secular history, Froude's, which is reappearing
just now, might be good. Have you read Living-

stone's? If not, you might get that for Sabbath. It is the most Christlike life I ever heard of, except Paul's."

When a friend asks us what books to read, or an invalid for a sudden accession of illness, or a traveller for a long journey, we should all have a répertoire, a list in memory's secret drawer to call out at once. First let us taste for ourselves, and then be a purveyor of good books. Very much depends on the time, the circumstance, the mood when a book is read. When we have read it and passed our verdict, did we give it a fair chance, did we give it our undivided attention? We remember a friend saying to us how much more profitable it was to read a book in one's own copy, which we could mark at will, than in a fugitive library copy. And we have found this to be increasingly true. Sometimes after making a book our own by marking, we have been tempted to leave it with a friend, and when we wanted it for reference it was gone. There is a moving population of summer visitors who come and go, and leave not much impression on our bit of land; but we must have some residenters living in mansions or villas who have taken a lease for life to purchase a place in our lives. Mr. Stead speaks of the "communion of readers," and such bonds are healthy and strong. In your friends' bookcases you have a key to their tastes, an index to their lives. You go with a friend on holiday. As is his habit he may have taken a book suitable to the district, such as Wordsworth at the Lakes, or Scott at Kenilworth, *Romola* in Florence; and as he turns the pages you know his thoughts. Leaving Marseilles, on two deck-chairs lay copies of *Monte Christo*.

The readers did not speak, being better employed, but though utter strangers, never again likely to meet, they were for the time friends. Certainly it is safer, when talking is resorted to, to discuss a book than a person. People get friendly over a book which they have both discovered to be to them "the most brilliant book of travel of the century"; and just when they have begun to read some standard book, they are pleased to see it praised in a magazine. The more they read, the more their reading seems to overlap like wave on wave on a pebbly shore, and the more they realise their own ignorance. How easy it is for the young to found a library, a bookcase of their very own, compared to what it was in our young days. There are the penny poets and the fourpenny standard novels within reach of all; and we have heard from a friend about a wonderful collection which can be got in Glasgow for the sum of six shillings, including postage.

Hugh Miller says: "I began to collect a library in a box of birch bark about nine inches square, which I found quite large enough to contain a great many immortal works;" and we know what his learning grew to. When a book is lent, it is a great help to put the name of the person to whom it has gone on a slip of paper on the shelf. A prize might be offered for the most effective punishment for the non-returning of books. The careful librarian will send out a reminder, a post-card, to recall it, or a reply post-card, asking when it will be returned; but it is the duty of the person who received the favour of the loan not to keep it beyond a due time, a week or a month. Some one said: "Though my friends are poor arithmeticians, yet they are good bookkeepers!" We know how great scholars treat their books, and we long to imitate them. They exercise great care and solicitude, and will let no stranger hands dust or disarrange. For a library is like a garden. It needs pruning; it needs weeding; it needs raking and watering, arrangement and rearrangement according to the plan which the proprietor feels most helpful to him.

Speaking of libraries, the well-known story comes to mind of one who was mostly concerned as to the outward appearance. He ordered his several shelves to be filled with volumes of varying size, and when asked if they were to be bound in russia or morocco, replied, "What's the use o' sending them so far; can they no' be bun' at hame?"

The young are very critical. We went with a friend who had literary tastes, and who had lived among books, into the study of a writer. What struck her was the meagreness of his library. Her standard was high. In another country house, very destitute of books, we found one which helped us. The owner was not aware that it was in the house. Next to the good done to the young by founding a library we would put the keeping of a book of extracts. True, it is asked, "Do you ever use them?" but the mere writing out of the lines impresses them on the memory. And then it is like the delight of arranging a vase of flowers to see those that go well together, and add new beauty each to the other. What rare delight it is to quarry a piece out of the solid rock yourself, instead of merely picking them from a heap of metal on the roadside. A list of pieces in a book of quotations is like eating bride-cake which causes indigestion, or to use merely a book of quotations, as if a dinner were all made up of savouries without substantial dishes. What a joy it is to share our treasures with some appreciative and enthusiastic friend. When on showing your notebook you can tell the habitat of the plant, and still more, that you plucked it and labelled it yourself, the joy is something akin to the botanist opening his herbarium, or the geographer making a new map. The author's name attached is like the hall-mark of the Queen's head on the silver, or the cock on the Cantigalli china. We would say to the children, "Save up your pennies for books rather than sweetmeats," and "learn by heart whilst yet the memory is nimble."

A book may bind a whole family together in loving sympathy if suited to be read on the different flats of a house. A friend has started a lending library to be put in servants' halls in country houses. The subscription is small, and the books are sometimes gladly welcomed upstairs. A douane and douanier should certainly be stationed at our bookshelves, not to let in any contraband literature. And who should seek to station this douanier like a mother? Lady Nairne began a book of extracts from books to leave for her son's use, but he went first. She had a high ideal in this as in all else, for one of her favourite mottoes was "Holiness is happiness." Mrs. Booth of the Salvation Army said to Mr. Stead: "Give us mothers; mothers are the want of the world." Some remember learning to read at their mother's side by the easy method of "Reading without Tears." In learning the alphabet they got a key to their mother's heart, and a strange life of interchange and communion began. On Sabbaths it was *Peep of Day* and *Line upon Line*, and afterwards *Ministering Children* was added to the list. The mother hears the child throw out a hint and acts on it, and at the next birthday or Christmastide prepares some surprise. A girl went to the country to nurse an invalid, and she found packed, by her mother's desire, among the clothing the blue volume sequel to *Ministering Children* which she had long desired to have. And when the treasured gift has an inscription with a loved quotation, or pages marked worthy of special study, the value of the gift is enhanced. After the Bible, which another cannot study for us, with its chapters learnt by heart, its tracks of waste land cultivated, and mines explored with help of Cruden (who seemed to our minds more a person than a book), what book was like the dear old "Pilgrim," as we called it. A student told us that there was hardly a Sabbath passed on which he did not read out of the *Pilgrim's Progress*, and it is to us the ideal book after the Bible. Then our mother arranged *Rutherford's Letters* for us on a plan of a letter, or part of a letter, for every day in the year. The attractive binding and beautiful paper of Andrew Bonar's edition first impressed us, but the book was ever a delight. Foremost among the favourite stories of our childhood stands *Robinson Crusoe*, and not far behind it the *Swiss Family Robinson*. In later days we have seen children devouring Ballantyne's *Coral Island*, which is somewhat akin. In a train to London we read *Uncle Tom's Cabin*. Across our memories there flit the images, the places where we read the books, the friends who gave them, and it is good to tell our children the histories that there is not time to write. In these days of deluges of literature, typewriting machines, of evening papers, of fountain pens, the hours seem to have fewer minutes and the days fewer hours; but with the scantier supply of children's books long ago there was just as much pleasure, and, perhaps, as much profit.

In later life it has been our privilege to make a study of some tracks of literature with one who was an authority and who had a master mind. We took each winter a different author for an hour's reading regularly and thoroughly: a course of Browning, including the "Ring and the Book," a course of Dante, one of Ruskin, and one of Wordsworth. We all have allocated different readings at different times, remembering some books along with the sunsets over the sea at country houses when they were read aloud in the long summer evenings. The good of this course of study was from the side-lights that the friend threw on the reading, as he explained the growth of the writer's mind, the source where he got certain ideas, etc. These talks favoured assimilation and digestion. We have come across his vigorous marginal pencillings this winter, now that his hand is cold in death. We only wish we had taken down notes of all he told us. In a course of reading he was like a living encyclopædia, for he knew the chief figures in the literature of the period.

Paul said "especially the parchments," and in our longing after the ideal in books, we feel that we are just like children throwing stones into the sea and listening to the waves which speak of the expanse beyond. For life is so short and the books so many that the difficulty is to remember what we have read and have it ready for use, and not as rusty weapons in an armoury.

And the most learned will tell you they are still at the beginning, though advancing. We watch with interest the growth of the mind of our friends. We may court introductions to the great and good, but we need not wait for an introduction to a book; and then, when tried and proved, it is our privilege to pass it on to others. A friend told us once that he did not understand Browning, but that he loved Mrs. Barrett Browning. Only the other day he advised us to read over again " Rabbi ben Ezra." His child had educated him. In our drawing-room Browning and Virchow discussed "Paracelsus" twelve years ago, but we hardly then knew Browning's poems, else how different would the conversation have been to us! It was Browning who said,

"Ah, but a man's reach should exceed his grasp,
  Or what's a heaven for?"

and each time we turn his pages our ideal is raised. For writers and readers alike we close this chapter with Milton's grand words. Let no young reader fear the long name, but go to the pages where he will find it for himself in the "Areopagitica." The effect that the words have on us as they call us from our low level and scrappy reading, are like leaving the hurdy-gurdy organ on the street and entering a great cathedral where the grand music is swelling out, and one by one the worshippers yield themselves to the spell—

"For Bookes are not absolutely dead things, but do contain a potencie of life in them to be as active as that soule was whose progeny they are ; nay, they do preserve as in a violl the purest efficacie and extraction of that living intellect that bred them. I know they are as lively, and as vigorously productive, as those fabulous dragons teeth ; and being sown up and down, may chance to spring up armed men. And yet, on the other hand, unlesse warinesse be us'd as good almost kill a Man as kill a good Booke ; who kills a man kills a reasonable creature, God's image ; but hee who destroys a good booke, kills reason itselfe, kills the Image of God, as it were in the eye. Many a man lives a burden to the earthe ; but a good booke is the pretious life-blood of a master spirit, imbalm'd and treasured up on purpose to a life beyond life."

CHAPTER XI

THE MISSIONARY IDEAL

"There was depression in every direction. We met and prayed for the heathen. We were drawn out of ourselves. God blessed us while we tried to be a blessing. Our hearts were enlarged, and we were baptized into a deeper sympathy with the soul-saving purposes of the Redeemer. And the spirit was contagious."—ANDREW FULLER.

"O Master! when Thou callest,
  No voice may say Thee nay,
For blest are they that follow
  Where Thou dost lead the way;
In freshest prime of morning
  Or fullest glow of noon,
The note of heavenly warning
  Can never come too soon.

> They who go forth to serve Thee,
>   We, too, who serve at home,
> May watch and pray together
>   Until Thy kingdom come;
> In Thee for aye united,
>   Our song of hope we raise,
> Till that blest shore is sighted,
>   When all shall turn to praise!"

ALREADY to some is it like the sound of the wheels of His chariot, the advent of His feet, the missionary ideal realised, "the world for Christ," when the cultured youth of all the nations are federating to "make Jesus King." And the news that comes to us from the ends of the earth is often like a page of some romantic story. We heard from a lonely missionary in the heart of Africa, whose faith is as great as his bodily strength is weak. It takes five months for a letter to go to him. It may arrive or not, according to the good luck the letters have at the hands of the carriers; though only the wrapper may arrive without the book. From his outlook the chariot may seem long of coming, but with what joy will the lonely sentinel months after hear of the Liverpool Conference! It would be worth while to have from him not a photograph of the face which we remember as more spirit than flesh, but of the innermost soul beating on all alone true for Christ and His heathen, having for his treasured possession a wife's grave. Surely a sight of that soul, so like the Master, treading the wine-press alone, would fire our icy coldness, for he is an ideal missionary. This is a part of his last letter—

"I do not know if you would remember a young wife of the king, in whose heart—and for more than two years—the grace of God had been working. Being a favourite wife, she was not free to leave the royal harem. Once, on a very solemn occasion, when several had made a profession, the king summoned her also to speak, for he knew the work that had gone on in her soul. But he meant that she might make a profession, and still hold her place as one of his concubines. She answered by a flood of silent tears. At last she entreated him not to stand in the way of her salvation, but to free her once for all. The king, who himself is wavering, would have liked, for reasons of his own, to postpone that step. But he yielded at last, and very nobly. By her own slaves he had all the material prepared for her house in the village ; and then last Sunday, when she stood up in church, and with a firm, clear voice declared herself a follower of Jesus, and made a short but pointed appeal to the chiefs, the whole congregation was breathless, and all eyes were fixed upon her. But soon they were fixed on the king himself, who had risen to his feet, and declared that it was with his fullest consent that that young woman left once for all his harem. And then, turning to the big chiefs, he said, 'It is useless to fight against the things of God,'—and taking an image from the course of the sun,—'they have risen: we cannot impede them and push them back. They must go forth.' This has caused a very great sensation. The chiefs were enraged. They declared the woman was mad. Why did she not wait for the king to become a Christian himself? Why set such an example to their own wives? Indeed, she has put our little world upside down. Meantime, she is no more a 'queen.' Nobody kneels now before her and claps hands as a few days ago, although she is of royal blood, a cousin of the king; but she is cheerful and happy,—she is free. A host of men and women have been after her to compel her to go back to the City of Destruction, but the Lord sustains her. Now we are waiting for the king himself."

As we write, a letter comes from India, saying—

"One of our hospital patients had been ill for long with chronic bronchitis. She was a woman of about fifty-five years, had been a Telegu Brahmin, but married a Mohammedan man, and broke caste. Her name was Raddia. One night her distress was terrible. Next day we found her sinking. Her mind was quite clear, and she spoke with joy in laboured sentences of going to be with Jesus Christ. She knew quite well that she was dying. She had no fear. She asked that she might be buried as a Christian woman, and regretted that she had not been baptized. My fellow-worker went to tell the missionary, and he at once said that he thought she should be baptized, and he would come to do it. We knew it would comfort her. It was a very simple and a very solemn service. The dying woman, fighting hard for breath, confessed her faith in Him who had brought life and immortality to light. She was baptized in the name of the Father, of the Son, and of the Holy Ghost. She could not speak much after that, but in whispered, broken sentences told us that her 'heart was very happy,' that she 'had peace.' Just about midnight that same night she fell on sleep."

A steamer is even now putting out from Bordeaux,

carrying back, for the second time, to the French Congo a choice labourer. With him as freight he carries a house, a boat, seeds for his garden, and, among his books, *Make Jesus King*. He knows the deadly nature of the climate, but if it is to finish there his course with joy, he counts not his life dear. In the gay city of Paris, as, long ago, in the upper room at Jerusalem, or in the Catacombs of Rome, a company of friends met to wish him God-speed; and two student friends have caught the enthusiasm, and are to follow to Africa.

One of the ideals of missionary life is consecration. We all know the breath of one of those souls upon us, the effect of one of their letters; and why are these consecrated spirits so rare? It does not need a Tent or a Conference; the Spirit is ours, and it may be said of any of us as it was long ago, " The Spirit of God clothed himself with Gideon." When they leave us the ordinary conversation of Christians seems cold, the discussions about lines of demarcation between the Church and the world so futile; for we have been with those who have seen the vision of Christ and the needs of the heathen world.

> " Whoso hath felt the Spirit of the Highest
> Cannot confound nor doubt Him, nor deny:
> Yea, with one voice, O world, though thou deniest,
> Stand thou on that side, for on this am I."

Our standard of life has been raised for a few days, and the heat or feeling of a room all depends on what you have come from. Some features have struck us in some ideal missionaries and workers we have known which may help us to make our missionary ideals real. We think of one who went about with no excitement or hurry. He failed to keep an appointment with us one forenoon for reading and prayer. Later on other duties were pressing, and he found the door locked. The words were called in, "I've been O. H. M. S." He meant "On His Majesty's Service." The service had been praying and talking with a needy soul in another room. It was business, and he meant it. Without unhealthy excitement there may be great enthusiasm; and this enthusiasm is infectious when it has been generated in the atmosphere of secret and social prayer. For the separated ones there is freedom, for His yoke is easy and His burden light.

Another thing we find in these ideal missionaries is the joy of sacrifice. They would not say it, but when we wondered why the serpent of trial had become a rod in their hand, and how that rod seemed to blossom for them, and every conversation had the flavour of eternity, every hymn was praise and every petition meant business, we felt that hidden deep in their heart was the motto, " He left all; rose up and followed Jesus." The sacrifice demanded of some such has been unto death, but they live on in thoughts like these penned in an outgoing steamer, "I have just passed Aden. Why was Ion Keith Falconer taken and I left?" The Holy Ghost is given to them that obey Him, and if the Spirit has His way He may make strange demands.

Ideal missionaries are all men of great faith.

> "Believe!" I say, "Faith is my waking life:
> One sleeps, indeed, and dreams at intervals,
> We know, but waking's the main point with us,
> And my provision's for life's waking part."

"And so you live to sleep as I to wake,
To unbelieve as I to still believe."

They are awake, and thank God for what is to be done before they see it. Mr. Radcliffe had a room prepared for anxious souls in a boarding-school, and the first person to walk in was the headmistress, who had just before objected to its being prepared. And with faith will always go the joyous, praising spirit. Ordinary Christians may call them fanatical. The day will declare when the wood, hay, and stubble will be burned up, and the gold of service will be left, and they are content to wait.

We feel towards the missionaries as to those who have got swift promotion in the ranks. We at home are only common soldiers. To the command, "Go," the risen Lord linked one of His sweetest promises, "I am with you all the days." We think of a brother and a sister. The brother died of cholera in China, but the missionary spirit of the sister who stayed at home was just as true, when she said to her lover, "Are you one who would sacrifice the greatest temporal for the smallest spiritual advantage?" We quote some lines from her pen about how the missionary life is to be lived at home and abroad: "When a merchantman sets sail for a foreign port, the partner at home feels that he has as much at stake as the captain on board. In the same way, when a missionary agrees to go abroad, it is much to be desired, nay, for the success of the undertaking, it is vital that some one in the old country should be brought to take as real an interest in the errand on which the other is going, as if he himself were, say, China bound. The worker at home must be led to give himself up to labour here in such a way, in sympathy so strong, in effort so active and judicious, as virtually to become set apart as a missionary." This makes us think of the way she entertained that ideal missionary, William Burns, at her home. "When we invited Mr. Burns to dinner, we received from him the usual reply, that his work and study took up all his time. He did not dine out, or even breakfast, anywhere; but he would call at the house. The call was a late one, and, as the dinner-bell sounded, Mr. Burns rose to leave. A man of simple habits, he was caught by guile. 'Sorry we cannot ask you to stay to dinner. We have only a sheep's head to offer you,' said his hostess. 'Oh,' was the ready answer, 'if you put it that way I shall stay! There's nothing I like better.'

"It was one day in September 1853 that the Scottish Auxiliary of the China Mission was set on foot. Miss ——, who had worked with her brother during his twenty years of congregational and mission work in England, and one of her brother's friends were of the party. At one of the pauses in conversation she said, as though half in fun, 'I think you two idle gentlemen might do worse than start a Scottish branch of our mission!' Probably the idea had been simmering in their minds long before; anyhow, prayer was there and then offered up for guidance. By October of the following year the first Annual Meeting of our Auxiliary was held. William Burns appeared on the scene from his seven years' term of service in time for it. It was his first and last visit to Scotland. He was asked if he never felt home-sickness in China. He promptly said, 'I never knew that feeling till now;' meaning that China was for him altogether home."

Many other missionaries at home on furlough have the same tale to tell. They have known the privations, the loneliness, the longings of the missionary life, but they have the home-sickness for the land of their adoption. Christ says, "Go ye into all the world;" "Look ye on the fields." Let us go with Him alone, and try to write the sum where He says, "How much owest thou?" Otherwise *He* will write our verdict on the palace wall of eternity—"Weighed in the balance and found wanting." We are living in the interval between His teaching the petition "Thy kingdom come," and the shout of triumph "The kingdoms of this world have become the kingdoms of our Lord and of His Christ." Constantly gaps are made in the ranks of missionaries, and we long for the wise counsel of the missionary-hearted stayers at home who are now with the Lord. They did their work, and though not allowed to see the fruition, we think of Sir Bartle Frere's conversation with the aged man, who was planting acorns. He thought his friend rather fanciful. "You feel that I shall never enjoy the shade?" "Yes." He replied, "I know what that shade will be, and, at anyrate, no one will ever alter these lines." We sit now in the shade of the great oaks planted by Carey and Brainerd, by Heber, William Burns, and Duff. They rest, but their works follow.

A saint, now with the Lord, used to call a child to watch the lovely golden sunset, or, later in the evening, the pink of the aurora borealis, saying how she longed that it might be the King coming. As we see everywhere the missionary enthusiasm lighting up our grey northern skies, we think the missionary ideal is slowly yet surely coming, and these words express our longing—

> " Lo, as some ship, outworn and overladen,
>   Strains for the harbour, where her sails are furled ;
> Lo, as some innocent and eager maiden
>   Leans o'er the wistful limit of the world,
>
> Dreams of the glow and glory of the distance,
>   Wonderful wooing and the grace of tears,
> Dreams with what eyes and what a sweet insistance
>   Lovers are waiting in the hidden years ;
>
> Lo, as some venturer, from his stars receiving
>   Promise and presage of sublime emprise,
> Wears evermore the seal of his believing
>   Deep in the dark of solitary eyes ;
>
> So even I, and with a pang more thrilling,
>   So even I, and with a hope more sweet,
> Yearn for the sign, O Christ ! of Thy fulfilling,
>   Faint for the flaming of Thine advent feet."

CHAPTER XII

THE IDEAL IN FELLOWSHIP

" How good it is to hail pilgrims on the great journey even for an hour by the way: the sound of their 'tramp, tramp' quickens one's own tread, and makes one take in his knapsack-strap one hole further."—R. W. BARBOUR.

ONE of the little songs of ascents which were sung as the tribes were going up to the temple, was Psalm cxxxiii.: " Behold, how good and how pleasant it is

THE IDEAL IN FELLOWSHIP

for brethren to dwell together in unity!" Like oil, like dew, for "*there* the Lord commanded the blessing, even life for evermore." There is heaven begun. God means us to be joined together. He hath set the solitary in families. We are not solitary atoms, nor wandering stars. We belong to a family, a church, a kingdom. "They that feared the Lord spake often one to another; and the Lord hearkened, and heard."

Outside our home-life many new and old agencies are promoting unity. When we heard lately of a Christian Endeavour band where fifty young people of the congregation were studying the Bible and praying aloud together, we did not wonder that the minister received ten young communicants as a definite result.

One bond is love, another prayer. Love makes perpetual summer in the soul, for it is an evergreen. Some travellers escape winter altogether, and find two springs, two summers, as they leave the South, come slowly North, and then leave with the swallows again. Where love is the atmosphere the other fruits of the Spirit quickly follow. Inconsiderateness of others, which is just selfishness, quickly disappears. William Law says if we have hard thoughts about any, let us pray for them, and then we begin to love. "What counsel give ye me to return answer to this people? And they spake unto him, saying, If thou be kind to this people, and please them, and speak good words to them, then they will be thy servants for ever." Prayer and love make harsh speaking impossible. A Highland minister, speaking of the woman who slipped in and washed Christ's feet with tears, said: "When Christians take to washing one another's feet, some use water so hot that it scalds us, others so cold that it freezes us; but hers was blood-heat." Dispositions are so different, environment is so varied, that each day we must learn to "praise more and blame less." He did not quench the smoking flax.

Love will never want outlets when it exists. We saw a friend not long ago in the south of France. Whether it was in reading a chosen chapter or verse from God's word, or making a cup of beef-tea, he seemed to live and carry with him an atmosphere of love. He told us that in a town among the mountains there was a cab proprietor who had been very kind and considerate to him. He did not tell him the day of his arrival, as he could count on the hotel omnibus being at the station; but he took out of the train a whip carefully wrapped up, which he had brought from England for his friend. To his amazement, when he got out of the station, who was seated on the box of his carriage, to give him a surprise and drive him home, but his friend. When two hearts meet who love, it is as a time of spate on two Highland rivers; they join with a rush of joy, and their force is doubled. This may seem a small and ordinary circumstance, but upon this spirit of love all unity is built up. "Better to build on foundations than on ruins." Could we have a more lovely foundation-stone to lay at any time than just this hundred and thirty-third Psalm? Besides love and prayer, two bonds of union in our homes are family worship and reverence for the Lord's day. Let us dig deep the channels of His appointment, and He will fill the pools. Let us see to it that the altar is in our home. It is our part to build it; He will send the fire to consume the sacrifice. The morning hymn at worship tunes the day. The evening children's hour on Sabbath may bring out instead of toys the missionary boxes (perhaps one still kept for the child now serving in the temple on high) and the Sunday album. It will be ill for him and for his household who despises God's Eden gift to our race, and breaks down the fence of the Sabbath day. Wild creatures will rush in and destroy his fields. The cares and the pleasures, the worries and the traffic of everyday life, will not easily be shut out again. This will come if the thoroughfare be opened and the boarding taken down, "No road this way." We read in a missionary magazine that Korea is establishing its Sabbath. Shall we cast ours away? Some find the "reading round" at worship still a help, and the occasional joining of all audibly in the Lord's Prayer. One of our valued friends and ministers, now at home with God, said that he found it of great use to have family worship at night, immediately after the evening meal of supper or dinner, so that all the children might be present and nobody be drowsy.

In the home-life there must be sympathy, exchange of books or gifts or news with those who, though serving us, are, like us, serving Christ. We are helped by remembering how the ideal in home-life was lived out by those now at home with God. When father and mother have both gone, one feels as if the roof over our head were gone, and that we must now become more than ever, to those growing up around us, what they are to us. As we sigh for them, Riley's lines to a child come to our mind—

> "There! little girl; don't cry!
> They have broken your heart, I know;
> And the rainbow gleams
> Of your youthful dreams
> Are things of the long ago;
> But heaven holds all for which you sigh.—
> There! little girl; don't cry!"

We cannot think of those who have gone without our ideal being raised. We have been made to drink into the same spirit. Why are there ever days of discord and friction in our souls, in our family life, in our social gatherings or meetings as Christians? "The fruit of the Spirit is love," and love is unity. We remember how on a dusty Boulevard between Cannes and Cannet, we wondered and rejoiced in the green palm-trees when the grass was brown and all else was burned up. One day we learned the secret. At the top of a slope a long piece of indiarubber pipe from a water-supply was being led into deep channels cut round each plant, with connecting channels from each in a straight line to the next. The water filled them, and the soil was shovelled in again to protect from the sun's rays. The plants revived. Where the Spirit of the Lord is, there is unity.

> "I thirst for springs of heavenly life,
> And here all day they rise;
> I seek the treasure of Thy love,
> And close at hand it lies;
> And a new song is in my mouth,
> To long-loved music set:
> Glory to Thee for all the grace
> I have not tasted yet."

CHAPTER XIII

THE IDEAL IN SUFFERING

"There are some far-travelled, bruised, and battered souls who will understand everything when they arrive."

THE garden has its rain-gauge, the river the measuring-pole for times of flood, the porch its thermometer, but who shall measure the heights and depths of pain, the sharp twinge, the dull, wearing-out, monotonous continuity, the long-drawn-out agony? As in a range of hothouses we pass from one to another, and feel the temperature rising to degrees that make us more and more sensitive to the outside chill, we see in successive compartments the forms of beauty and wealth of sweetness increase; so is it in the experience of God's choicest saints. There are the every-day hardy plants, but the grape-clusters and the orchids need much heat. The gardener's stock of coal diminishes, the luxuriance increases. In a back room in Naples Bishop Lightfoot went in to see a sufferer. A maiden as kind and skilful as that of Naaman's wife with her strange tongue had been trying a remedy. His cordial was, "No pain, no gain." As the writer of the Epistle to the Hebrews says: "It became Him, for whom are all things, and by whom are all things, in bringing many sons unto glory, to make the Captain of their salvation perfect through sufferings." And suffering becomes one of the steps to the perfection of His followers. Michael Angelo says: "Nothing makes the soul so pure, so religious, as the *endeavour* to create something perfect." We may be sure that Christ not only sends the suffering, but that He is with us in it, though the "form of the Fourth" with us in the fire may be hard to distinguish. It may not be till after the pain has gone that we see the Hand that smites; yet some of His chosen ones have sung, like Paul and Silas with the irons on, in the prison. Here is the heading of one of Miss Havergal's poems, written when climbing a hill of sorrow: "A Song in the Night, written in Severe Pain"—

> "I take the pain, Lord Jesus,
>   From Thine own hand;
> The strength to bear it bravely
>   Thou wilt command.
>
> I am too weak for effort,
>   So let me rest,
> In hush of sweet submission,
>   On Thine own breast."

Very often with saints less disciplined than she was, the first feeling is rebellion. They realise that they are caged birds with their wings cut. Engagements have to be cancelled, and the brain that wants to work is like wood or pulp, or the limbs are powerless to obey it. Why has this come? A child had slipped into a room where the doctor was vaccinating a baby-brother. She heard the scream and saw the blood, but never guessed from what dangers the lancet-prick would save the infant. All day the feeling of revenge against the minister of healing smouldered like fire, until at night she prayed that God would punish the doctor who hurt her little brother. And we feel this too. Worse to bear than our bodily suffering, be it an acute illness or the

harder trial of prolonged weakness, is our lot when
we have noiselessly to shut the door, or close a shutter,
leaving our dearest to the mystic sacrament of pain.
Then, indeed, is our frail barque out from the pier,
away from the harbour, rocked on the billows in a
heavy, seething sea, compass and rudder lost. In
each case, for watcher or sufferer, the amount and
degree vary according to the temperament and frame
of the person. No diver has brought up correct
soundings of any human heart, no plummet has
measured aright the depth of human feeling. We
think of the lines of the poet—

> "Souls by nature pitched too high,
> By suffering plunged too low."

All through the Bible it is not so much deliverance,
though Christ loved to grant it, and went about healing all manner of sickness and disease, that is sought
for and gained, as His realised presence granted to
the sufferer. Paul says: "I besought the Lord thrice,
that it might depart from me. And He said unto
me, My grace is sufficient for thee: for My strength
is made perfect in weakness." Christ said: "If it be
possible, let this cup pass from Me: nevertheless not
as I will, but as Thou wilt." Dante's sentence has
been to many as a life-line thrown out for their hope
and rescue from all doubts and misgivings. "In His
will is our tranquillity." Thus wrote a friend to
a sufferer: "Three years are well spent in learning
Dante's line—

> 'In la sua volontade è nostra pace.'

Time does not make people better, nor trial, nor
sorrow, but only submission to His will; and these

have but one thing to teach, and it is that. When it is learnt we really have done with these."

Faith sees His will paramount, and for the time faith makes the other things non-existent. Some travellers had driven to Grindelwald and spent the day in exploring that bewitching neighbourhood. All the way there and back they desired to see one peak, of which they had so often heard. Just as they were nearing home the mist lifted, and the rosy evening light lit up the Jungfrau, and it dwarfed all else. The vision of the Will of God, higher even than service, is an epoch in any life. If His will is first, instead of the longed-for desire, the coveted object, a change occurs which would have before seemed impossible; but our sun colours the plants, our winter gives place to spring, the moon claims kinship with the tides, the tempest is quiet at His command, the age of miracles is not yet past. As Augustine says: " It is not by our feet, or change of place, that men leave Thee, or return unto Thee." His promises, His verilies, are as sheet-anchors at such times. There was one who lived to do kindnesses, and she had a patent of her own. When friends were going long voyages she put a series of envelopes, one inside another, with dates attached, so that they might have a message of cheer from her at different stages, or at times when they felt lonely. More surely and more freshly does our Father send straight from Himself the word we need. He knows the weary nights when in the stillness one longs for morning. God intends sleep to be the time of repose, the easy bridge from one day to another. He does not want His waiting-room to be turned into a workshop; but when He withholds the sleep He is there to soothe the restlessness. And we always have the company of those whom one has called the night-watchers in the temple, the many sick in lonely room or hospital, the great company of those for whom our night is day in other quarters of the globe.

But for the most part we rejoice in knowing that we suffer alone with Him. In His book all our members are written, all the limitations, all the disappointments. He is the Head, and though He allows no stranger to regulate the furnace heat or mould the clay, yet when one member suffers all the members suffer. And how hard it is to lose some of the members of the earthly body when they go to make up the heavenly. It is as sore as losing one of the members of our earthly tabernacle. Who shall solve the problem of the early dead, and the limitation of suffering imposed on the most useful who are left? "In His will is our peace." "Most gladly therefore will I rather glory in my infirmities." They go on before to prepare the place for us, and He will keep His "tryst in the Valley" with us. It has been said that only one thing is certain, that we shall all die. We add that only one thing is sadder, that is the sin that causes death. The moral pain of having done wrong, and yielded to sin, has led many to realise that the hell of the future, to be alone with an impenitent heart and a living conscience, might be worse than any actual flame or gnawing worm. Each one has to suffer alone and die alone ; but it is in hours of strength and relief from pain that we must face the future, and acquaint ourselves with Him and be at peace. Now is the time to make a confidant of Him who " knoweth our flittings," who makes paths in the sea, who makes mountains a way, and bare heights pastures, who alone doeth wonders. In the hour of sickness and death other necessities come trooping in, and this dissolving body clamours for attention.

Let us be willing scholars in His school, arriving, though it may be slowly, at this ideal—the knowledge of His will. The holidays will soon come, when the Ideal will be real in His presence. These lines of Adelaide Procter seem to us like a lifeboat sent out to us amid the wreckage of wasted hours or opportunities. If we enter it, we shall be landed in the harbour, and already the rainbow spans the rain-clouds, as to the sufferer, her message is—

> " Have we not all, amid life's petty strife,
> Some pure ideal of a noble life
> That once seemed possible? Did we not hear
> The flutter of its wings, and feel it near,
> And just within our reach? It was. And yet
> We lost it in this daily jar and fret,
> And now live idle in a vague regret.
> But still *our place is kept*, and it will wait,
> Ready for us to fill it, soon or late:
> No star is ever lost we once have seen,
> We always may be what we might have been."

CHAPTER XIV

BEHOLDING OUR IDEAL

"We live in a very busy, perspiring time, when a thousand clamant calls assail us on every side; but we must have more time for visions if we would be well equipped for tasks."

SOME years ago there lived with us in a country house one whose personality made us always think of the Apostle John, and when we heard that Dr. Gordon of Boston had passed away, the world seemed poor indeed. His face was finely chiselled under the white hair, and there was deep experience in it; peace had come after storms and striving, and love filled it. Children and all loved him. Outside on the iron staircase there was a wealth of sweet-briar; inside his presence was like perfume poured out. This is what we wrote down to his dictation: "Evangelical faith consists not only in a glance, but also in a gaze. A single glance is sufficient to save, but a prolonged gaze is necessary to sanctify." Another friend tells us that where we read, "We beheld His glory," it is literally we "*theatrised* His glory—prolonged our delighted gaze upon it, as the Greeks did with the masterpieces presented in the theatre, detaching themselves from all other occupations, and surrendering themselves to all the impressions of the hour." This is the spot where ideals are generated, this is the atmosphere where saints are made. Let us each so live as that we shall be entitled to the name which legend ascribes to the beloved disciple, *Epistethios*, the leaner upon the breast. "Multitudes are ready to speak for Christ, or to sacrifice themselves in labouring for His cause. But the utterances are too few that come from sitting at His feet, or leaning on His breast." The communion with Him takes different forms, according to the temperament and condition of the person, but the Spirit is the Revealer, the Unveiler. With some it is as the infant's cry, the whisper from a sickbed; with the young and vigorous it is the "strong crying with tears," the wrestling to obtain. One thus describes it: "The soul is sighing; for the vision tarries: and we grudge even the brief threescore and ten years that separate us from the goal. Is this only a dim and tantalising vision, this knowledge of our bad selves and revelation of our better selves? Does the Eternal bind us so intolerably in the irons of time? We pant, we crave, we fret, in passionate prayer, we plead to be allowed to touch if only with the tip of the finger the glorious and entrancing realities of the world beyond. And while we pray, from the midst of the Timeless rises the To-day, from the midst of the Spaceless rises the Here, and a sight of the Father opens our eyes till we see our Brother: the Ideal has now descended from heaven."

"We beheld His glory." Faith is the eye, Hope is the field-glass to bring the distant near. "Without faith it is impossible to please Him." But there is a germ working havoc in us all; it is like a cancer eating out the life. It is unbelief. It empties the promises, sours the psalms, and vitiates all. Even Christ could not do many mighty works because of their unbelief. If we analyse the proceedings of any one day—the engagement of a servant, the journey by cab, railway, or steamer, the buying of our daily provisions—we shall see what a large share faith has in every little transaction, and yet on the highest and most vital of all transactions we do not give it full play or power. But once we have beheld the Christ through saving faith, all other visions and sights for us are dwarfed. We felt how we must stay long and gaze on Niagara, and ponder over the Pyramids till their greatness dawned on us; and so it is with this greatest sight of all. We feel our own smallness, our own vileness. Isaiah did so when "he saw His glory." A strange attraction draws us back again to gaze and gather strength, and we long to copy His likeness. Two of the ripest saints we knew kept these mottoes over their mantelpieces, one from the Old Testament and one from the New, but both of the same purport: "Thou remainest;" "Jesus only."

It was the punishment in Dante's dream for those who would not look up when they might, to have always their backs and heads bent down. Let us so commend Christ that the strivings shall be generated in some young hearts to look past all the "vanity" (evanescence, not necessarily viciousness) of the things seen. "I am often compelled," says a correspondent, "to stop and wonder whether close study of any one subject does not so fix our eyes upon the ground and upon one point of truth, that we not only become narrow in our sympathies, and unable to appreciate other minds, but to lose the power of lifting our faces to the blaze of eternal light, which is the Reason and the End of all the rest. Even more difficult than study itself is the keeping of study in its right place as a handmaid in the outer courts of the King's Palace of Truth. I have often felt myself like one who ought to be swinging a censer before the altar of His presence, when in reality I am burning sacrifices to a pagan deity—rather to a whole Olympus of them. I suppose the only remedy is strictly to subject everything to the Lord of Light, so that things may be seen in their proper proportions, and we may not mar the eternal harmonies."

A young believer was distressed because of her difficulties. Like many others, she longed to wake up and find herself sanctified. So her French pastor wrote: "Avant tout, ma chère enfant, laissez-moi vous dire que vous n'êtes pas une exception, ce qui vous arrive est arrivé à beaucoup de chrétiens et des meilleurs. Si d'autres ont triomphé, vous triompherez aussi, si vous souffrez de cet état, et si vous desirez en sortir. Seulement ne vous figurez pas triompher une fois pour toutes, et ne soyez pas étonnée si vous traversez de nouvelles phases d'obscurité. La vie chrétienne n'est pas une crise d'un jour donnant naissance à un état de santé parfaite; c'est une lutte, ou, si vous le voulez, un travail de chaque jour, dont l'éternité seule verra le parfait achèvement."

So she tells us she is waiting and working till she shall awake "satisfied," like the Japanese workman who was parted from a loved piece of work. He let it go, looked up, and said, "The next will be more beautiful!" We wait for Eternity's fulfilment of our Ideal. "When He shall appear we shall be like Him; for we shall see Him as He is."

> "Fear not to build thine eyrie in the heights
>   Where golden splendours stay.
> And trust thyself unto thine utmost soul
>   In simple faith alway.
> And God will make divinely real
> The highest form of thine ideal."

CHAPTER XV

THE IDEAL LIFE

"HEAVEN.—the land where there are no two hemispheres, but only one infinite circle of united love."

"There is a beyond, and he who has once caught a glimpse of it is like a man who has gazed at the sun. Wherever he looks, everywhere he sees the image of the sun. Speak to him of finite things, and he will tell you that the finite is impossible and meaningless without the infinite. Speak to him of death, and he will call it birth; speak to him of time, and he will call it the mere shadow of eternity."

As the rose in the rose-bud, as the oak in the acorn, as the butterfly in the chrysalis, so surely lies the immortal hidden in our mortal frame. There is no waste in Nature, and even out of gas-refuse bright colours come; and is it possible to think of the Creator's works not coming to perfection in a future state?

What tries some minds most is the element of change in this life. Friends change and die: a residence abroad for some years makes you even feel your place in the home circle different when you return, and we change too. Not only does science grow apace and text-books change, so that there are new names and terms and newly-discovered facts about everything, but we also change. We grow out of books and experiences as out of clothes. Is it not the stirring of the immortal within us? A poor London child went for the day to the country, and came back saying, "I saw a bird and it had no cage." We sometimes leave our cages to try to walk or fly, but are forced back again by the limits of the things seen. But the vision seen by John of the New

Jerusalem coming down from God out of heaven, arrests our gaze. If we lived more in sight of this vision, there would not be such a crash or stoppage of the machinery of our life when one and another pass into it. For the Spirit, the Paraclete, is with us and them, and as the Psalm says so beautifully, Death is just the Shepherd who introduces into the Spirit World. We shall exclaim, even after all His revealings, "The half has never been told." It is said that Watts painted a picture of Covent Garden Market, which was strikingly beautiful. A visitor said: "Well, Mr. Watts, this is all very beautiful, but I know Covent Garden Market, and I have never seen it look like this." "But don't you wish you could?" the painter replied. The Spirit draws no picture for us that is only an imagination. It is all fact and reality.

> "Saints' deaths do but give dating to the world,
> They are the human points of that one plan
> Which moves unhindered and unhelped of man."

. To how many have the first stirrings of the ideal come because they wished to follow where the loved have gone. Like a cutting seen from a railway train, they had, down through the dark avenue of time, a vision of the city descending from God, and they set out in search of this ideal. "Now they desire a better country, that is, an heavenly." On occasions of great joy or sorrow or perplexity, we cannot help longing to have the loved ones at our side again, and our thoughts find expression in the words—

> "If I could call you back for one brief hour,
> It is at evensong that hour should be,
> When bells are chiming from an old grey tower
> Across the tranquil sea.

> Just when the fields are sweet and cool with dew,
> Just when the last gold lingers in the West,
> Would I recall you to the world you knew
>   Before you went to rest.
>
> And where the starry jasmine hides the wall,
> We two would stand together once again;
> I know your patience—I would tell you all
>   My tale of love and pain.
>
> I would not call you back; and yet, ah me!
> Faith is so weak, and human love so strong,
> That sweet it seems to think of what might be
>   This hour at evensong."

We walk between "the silences of the stars above and the graves beneath." Our loved ones would not return if they could. They wait for us on the heights, and surely are not idle. And if we asked the Spirit more He would commune with us more of the life beyond. In a forest in France a tourist called at an artist's studio, and after admiring the masterpieces, wanted to give a gratuity to the servant, when he found it was the artist himself. So gentle and dove-like are these breathings that we may not realise in whose company we are, till in the silence of a death-chamber, or rather a robing-room, His voice is heard. His name is Comforter. We have got so accustomed to the name that we miss the meaning and do not see the beauty. In the margin of the Revised Version another reading for Comforter is Helper; and that is what we need when the chamber is darkened and the heart stricken. More tenderly than a mother's hand does for her infant, will He at the same time let in the sunlight of eternity and yet not allow the glare to dazzle us. The French reading of the Psalm thus beautifully describes the place where the still small voice is heard: "Celui qui habite dans la retraite secrète du Souverain est logé à l'ombre du Tout-Puissant."

Not only in the quiet stillness, but in the busy thoroughfare of the crowded cities, we are on the confines of the eternal world. A military band was playing under a canopy in a foreign town Weber's "Invitation à la Valse." During a quick movement the musicians stopped for a space, and all heads were quickly uncovered; for as the crowd turned they saw a hearse bearing the coffin of a well-known citizen. Even as we write, the gay dancers in the ballroom one evening have to attend a Requiem Mass next morning for the sufferers in the terrible tragedy at Moscow. At such a time the gaze of the world is turned to what is going on daily in unrecorded ways; sorrow treading on the heels of joy. On one of the most beautiful spots on the Riviera, not far from Monte Carlo, one of the most sorrowful of sights is to be seen. A visitor thus describes it—

"There is a very sad sight to be witnessed at Monaco, about a mile from the rooms—the Suicides' Cemetery. It is situated above and apart from the ordinary burial-ground, in barren, uncultivated land, very much in keeping with its dire associations; and there are buried without ceremony any who have taken their lives through their losses at the Casino. Four blank walls forming a square enclose it, and the unfortunate one's resting-place is only marked by a piece of plain wood with a number on it. As the numbers only reach a little over thirty, one is apt to take comfort in thinking that there are not very many suicides; but when you are informed that the bodies are removed after a certain time, a feeling of dreadful depression comes." Did they pass away without God, without hope? Before they took the fatal plunge were they inquiring—

> "What of the Darkness? Is it very fair?
> Are there great calms, and find ye silence there?
> Like soft shut lilies all your faces glow
> Like some strange peace our faces never know,
> With some great faith our faces never dare;
> Dwells it in Darkness? Do ye find it there?
>
> Is it a Bosom where tired heads may lie?
> Is it a Mouth to kiss our weeping dry?
> Is it a Hand to still the pulse's leap?
> Is it a Voice that holds the runes of sleep?
> Day shows us not such comfort anywhere.
> Dwells it in Darkness? Do ye find it there?"

With deep thankfulness we turn from such a picture to find ourselves still with an open Bible, still with an Easter Morn reminding us that our Saviour Jesus Christ hath "abolished death, and brought life and immortality to light through the gospel." How shall we prepare for the ideal life? "The best way to practise dying is to practise living. Dying faith is just living faith. When the last signal is given, he who has lived well has nothing to do but die." We often long that Christ had told us more about the life beyond the grave; but we know that "His servants shall serve Him: And they shall see His face." One day in autumn, a large steamer, which had come from the Cape of Good Hope, entered Southampton Docks. The gangway was put down, and the passengers were eager to step on English soil. Setting foot on the gangway, we were stopped by an official coming on board, saying, "Wait till I get a clean bill of health from the captain." "There shall in no wise enter into it anything that defileth, neither whatsoever worketh abomination, or maketh a lie; but they which are written in the Lamb's book of life."

"The ideal stuff that is in a man, the something which hovers round him as a spirit of eternity—it is this which makes this world tolerable, and in the heart of it credible to us. It was really not worth while making a creature like man except this ideal world lay on the horizon of him, except he was in training for idealities; except this life is the rough scaffolding by which he reaches the home of them in God." This makes us sing with Whittier—

" I have but Thee, my Father! let Thy Spirit
    Be with me then to comfort and uphold;
No gate of pearl, no branch of palm I merit,
    Nor street of shining gold.

Suffice it if—my good and ill unreckoned,
    And both forgiven through Thy abounding grace—
I find myself by hands familiar beckoned
    Unto my fitting place.

Some humble door among Thy many mansions,
    Some sheltering shade where sin and striving cease,
And flows for ever through heaven's green expansions
    The river of Thy peace.

There, from the music round about me stealing,
    I fain would learn the new and holy song,
And find at last, beneath Thy trees of healing,
    The life for which I long."

FROM THE PORTRAIT OF SIR J. Y. SIMPSON

Painted for Mrs. Barbour by Norman Macbeth, R.S.A. A Replica in the Royal Maternity and Simpson Memorial Hospital was presented from the "Woman's Offering" Fund, initiated by Mrs. Barbour.

www.ingramcontent.com/pod-product-compliance
Lightning Source LLC
Chambersburg PA
CBHW032244080426
42735CB00008B/996